The Gowganda Pilot and Me

Our Survivals

The Gowganda Pilot and Me

Our Survivals

By Pat Craig

Copyright © 2014 by Pat Craig

*The Gowganda Pilot
and me, our survivals*
by Pat Craig

Printed in the United States of America

Edited by Xulon Press

ISBN 9781498403917

All rights reserved solely by the author. The author guarantees all contents are original and do not infringe upon the legal rights of any other person or work. No part of this book may be reproduced in any form without the permission of the author. The views expressed in this book are not necessarily those of the publisher.

Layout and cover design by Artiste Interactive
www.artisteinteractive.com
Littleton, Colorado

If you would like to contact the author, you may reach her through the book website: www.thegowgandapilot.com

www.xulonpress.com

TABLE OF CONTENTS

1. The Gowganda Pilot 13
2. The Cabin 19
3. From Beaver To Akron 23
4. Good News 33
5. Gone Fishing 43
6. The Plunge 51
7. Rescued 57
8. Going Ashore 63
9. At The Hospital 69
10. Back To The Cottage 75
11. Break Down 83
12. The Long Trip Home 111
13. Home At Last 119
14. Where's Charley 129
15. The Bicentennial 135
16. Closed In 141

17. Follow The Road..................... 151
18. Big Heart, Big Trouble 155
19. Dave And Angie 163
20. The Last Chapter.................... 173

Epilogue 183
The Gowganda Pilot 185

DEDICATION

To my father Jerry Dever who's strength, determination and presence of mind saved my son's, my husband's and my life. We are truly grateful.

Acknowledgements

Destiny determined that Edna Ogle and I would meet. It has caused our paths to come together in our glorious, golden years. I am very grateful for her as she is the one who has continued to be an inspiration to me, encouraging me to tell my story that is contained in this book. Thank you Edna.

Also, I thank my Creative Writing instructor, Danielle Steinfeld, at The Apex Center in Arvada, Colorado.

Some old photographs, courtesy of my cousin, Ron Dever.

1

THE GOWGANDA PILOT

My dad was always a very good pilot; he was not one to take chances but always cautious and thorough. He kept a handwritten checklist taped above the window of the cockpit to prevent skipping a single step in preparing for a flight. This however is a story that includes a certain flight that was destined to be a challenging situation for even the most experienced pilot, no matter what preparations were taken. I have never faulted Dad for what happened that day, due to the difficult and unusual circumstances. The problem was glassy water which can result in tragedy, more about that later.

I was nine years old in 1947 when Dad first started going to Gowganda, Ontario Canada. This was before he had his first airplane. In that era, that far north was unmapped and pictures were taken from 20,000 feet so there was very little detail on the maps. That kind of wilderness appealed to my dad. It must be something that is ingrained in all true outdoorsmen.

Art Smead, a friend of my dad who was a taxidermist in Cuyahoga Falls, Ohio (in Akron it is referred to as The Falls), had a camp in Gowganda and persuaded Dad to visit the camp for a fishing vacation. Outdoorsmen described Art as a man's man: self-sufficient, intelligent, and someone you would want with you if you were ever lost in the wilderness. Dad frequently studied books on surviving in the wilderness and enjoyed sharing his knowledge with others. It would naturally be necessary reading for a pilot in Canada, or anyone who lived in that country.

Art, and his wife Ruth, would occasionally invite us to their house in the Falls. Ruth was a gracious hostess and very sweet to me. They didn't have any children, so maybe that's why she paid so much attention to me. On one of my birthdays she took me to Yeager's in downtown Akron for the sole purpose of buying me a birthday present. I was to choose what I wanted and strangely enough, I remember that it was a multi-stripped, stretchy tank top. "Are you sure that's what you want?" she asked sweetly.

"Oh yes," I replied. I hope I thanked her. Young children don't always fully comprehend the thoughtfulness of an adult's gesture. Later in life, as we comprehend it, we wish we had been more expressive in our gratitude.

I remember so well, a table in a corner of her living room. It was round with tripod legs with ball and claw feet. It was covered with a crocheted square that she had carefully and beautifully made. Of special interest to me was the small clear crystal bowl filled with lemon drops that were always there. Since then, lemon drops have been one of my favorite hard candies. Today, guests will find them in my home in a small, clear, crystal bowl in memory of Ruth. *Thank you Ruth.*

Ruth had a small, copper-colored Chihuahua named Penney, such an appropriate name. It was obvious Ruth loved that cute, little dog. Dad never liked animals and was critical of how she fussed over her dog. I've read several quotes from different people regarding love for animals: "One's soul in not complete until they experience a love for animals." After all, our heavenly father created them first.

Most of Dad's life, he enjoyed hunting for trophies he could hang on the walls: bighorn, mountain sheep and goats, antelope, bear, deer, elk, and moose. That was the popular thing then with outdoorsmen. I don't think it is so much now. Later in life he lost the desire for it, saying, he could see it wasn't the thing to do – just for trophies. Those were always my thoughts. Putting food on the table is a different matter and in Gowganda, moose is often their beef, so to speak.

Well, the fishing results while staying at Art's camp were very favorable, enough so that he had his limit of pickerel in just three days. Dad was hooked (a small pun). Art put them in his ice house to keep them until we left at the end of the week. The "Ice House" was a shed filled with large blocks of ice, cut from the lake the winter before. Large deliveries of sawdust from the lumber mill were poured over the blocks to insulate them. This was effective enough to keep most of the ice all summer long.

We spent every vacation there after that summer except one, a trip to Washington, D.C., and that was the result of my whining, "Can't we ever go anywhere else besides Gowganda?" I have to assume he listened.

Gowganda has some interesting history. In 1907, prospectors discovered silver in the area of Gowganda and the small town became quite a thriving, boom town with men, sometimes bringing their families coming from everywhere to prospect for silver. It was an exciting era for the isolated community. After veins of silver became more difficult to find, prospecting greatly slowed and the population dwindled. People left to look for employment elsewhere.

The Great Boreal Forest covers the northern part of Canada. Within that is the Temiskaming Provincial Forest and deep within that lies Gowganda, 360 miles north of Toronto. Gowganda is in the heart of the lumber industry surrounded by the forests and has now become a major platform for the mining exploration that is going on west of town.

When we started going there, there was a large lumber mill somewhere on the southeast shore. Lumber trucks would bring in loads of timber most every day. I loved the smell of fresh cut pine when driving by the mill. Often, a few logs would get loose and drift to the north shore building up at the dam. I remember looking at them and wondering if I could walk across them, but being a cautious person, I chose not to.

2

THE CABIN

I was about nine when Dad bought a very small two-room, very rustic cabin outside of Gowganda. It was about this time he and a friend, Paul Stanley, co-owned a Seabee, an amphibian plane. The concept of an amphibian is a good idea however, upon learning more about it they decided it was not for them or their situation. If there is engine trouble resulting in engine failure, the plane has a very short gliding ratio.

The cabin was deep in the thick forest of pine and white bark birch trees. There wasn't even a road to it, just a very rough, path-like trail. The cabin couldn't have been very old because when I first walked in I remember it smelled so-o-o good. The walls were constructed of pine boards and they emitted a wonderful pine aroma. There was a screened-in front porch which was later ripped apart by a bear scavenging for food because Dad had thoughtlessly left groceries on the porch. He never did that again.

At that time there was no electricity in the area, at least not to the cabin. We had to use Coleman Lamps to provide ample illumination. Drinking and cooking water was drawn from the lake. It was that pristine. Bringing water to the cabin was my chore. Dad said it would help build my muscles. Of course, we had a little "house of necessity" in the back with a board walk to it to avoid walking through the brush.

Bathing was done in the lake, in a bathing suit, of course. The water was always cold, so we took our baths as quickly as possible. Coming out of the water we would always check ourselves for thirsty leeches that might be attached. There would usually be one or two on me. You don't just pull them off. First off, it would be very difficult and if you did, it would leave the teeth and mouth in the flesh. Lovely thought isn't it? We always kept a box of salt handy to sprinkle on them, causing them to immediately drop off. Occasionally, someone might be around who would have a lighted cigarette and just a touch of the lighted end would make them drop. Cigarettes are good for something it seems.

There were times we needed to go into a larger town like New Liskeard or Kirkland approximately sixty miles away. We would have to drive the one lane road through the forest leading out of Gowganda. It was a very rocky, winding dirt road, much of it over bedrock. I am told people traveled it hoping that they would not meet an oncoming car. If they did, the drivers would get out, flip a coin to determine who was going to back up to a point where the cars could squeeze by, and sometimes that could be quite a ways. Sometimes I think that someone made up that story. But, I enjoy telling it because it always gets a laugh.

Many times driving this road, we would see deer, bear, beautiful grosbeak birds, and moose. On one of our fishing outings a moose was crossing the lake and swam right across the bow of our boat. We thought that was pretty exciting. Over the years, Gowganda provided me with many memories. Memories filled with many experiences – some wonderful and exciting, and some terribly tragic and traumatic.

3

FROM BEAVER TO AKRON

Long before Gowganda, Dad and his parents struggled in the Great Depression as so many people did in those difficult and challenging days. He quit school in the ninth grade to financially help the family. He and his younger brother walked the railroad tracks for miles searching for coal that had fallen from the steam engines. He shoveled snow, washed windows, and swept floors, anything to generate income. He had a very strong work ethic even then. He once said that being broke was a good motivator to hit the bricks and find work.

Born in Jackson, Ohio the family moved to Springfield when he was about sixteen. At the age of seventeen he found a job selling popcorn at the boxing matches where he met a very pretty, young blonde from Tennessee who had moved to Springfield, Ohio to live with her older sister Billie. Later Mother and Dad eloped to Indiana to be married since they were too young to be married in Ohio according to Ohio's laws.

Twelve months later I was born in the small apartment they rented in Springfield down the street from Wittenberg College. It's hard to believe, but in those days doctors made house calls. My bed was in a dresser drawer and for years my dad would tease me by telling me that when I would cry they would close the drawer. I was convinced for a long time that story was true until my grandfather told me it wasn't so.

In 1942 we moved to Akron, Ohio so Dad could find employment. It was a wise decision because coming out of the Depression, Akron was a booming city. Thousands came from all over the country.

Goodyear Aircraft, Goodyear Tire, B.F. Goodrich, Firestone, General Tire and Mohawk Rubber all had factories in Akron, making Akron the rubber center of the world. There were many other prosperous corporations such as Burkhart Steel, Morton Salt, Saalfield Book Publishers, and many more.

People could walk in off the street and be hired on the spot. Dad was hired at Goodyear Aircraft and soon became a foreman. Many of the men at the plants were drafted or joined the armed forces for the war effort so more men were needed in the plants which made room for the "Rosie Riveters." Men with families were not drafted until late in the war.

I was very young during the war but, some things are very vivid in my memory such as the black-outs and the civil defense men in their white, metal hats. One of them came to our door in a black-out and told us to turn off the Christmas tree lights. Mother would take me with her to the Akron Armory to get her rations for food and gasoline for the car. I was about four years old at the time and remember her camel colored coat as I stood behind her. Women sacrificed their nylons for the production of parachutes and wore leg make-up instead. Nylons had seams at the back of the leg and some women actually drew a line on their leg to look like they had on the real thing.

I have outstanding memories of the end of the war. One is, the day I walked to my grandparent's house and saw her and an aunt sitting on the front steps, aprons drawn to their faces, dabbing their eyes, crying as though it was the end of the world. Well, it wasn't, it was the end of the war. That day a huge crowd of people paraded down Main Street in celebration of that marvelous event. There was a large, front page picture of the crowd and I was in there somewhere. I was there marching with them in my bare feet and remember stepping on a hot man-hole cover, hot from the burning August sun. Everyone thought it would be the end of all wars. Wouldn't that have been wonderful? Little did we know then how endless the wars would be in the future.

Soon after that, my grandmother asked me to come to the house. She said she had a surprise for me. When I walked through the door she motioned for me to follow her. "Come down to the basement," she said. "I want to show you something." I thought at the time it was strange that she wanted to show me something in the basement, which was more like a cellar. What would be in the basement that I would want to see?

As I walked towards the coal furnace, this fantastically, handsome, smiling man came walking toward me smiling broadly with white shining teeth. I was so stunned, my jaw must have dropped to my chest and I squealed at the striking vision I was seeing. He was very tall, blond, very tanned with piercing blue eyes, dressed in his white, white sailor uniform. It was my uncle Bob who served in the Pacific arena. He gave me the biggest hug....it was wonderful. I was deliriously happy. I clung to his side all that day and he didn't seem to mind.

Parents that had a son or daughter in the war effort put a small banner with a star in a front window for all to see. At one time, late in the war, my grandparents had five of those banners in their window. No wonder mom was crying when the announcement came that the war was over. She expected all of them to return home, and thankfully, they did all return safely. They were very fortunate though thousands were not.

*Thank you for your sacrifice
to keep America free.*

GOODYEAR

Goodyear Aircraft has an interesting history. In 1917 the company was known as the Goodyear Zeppelin Company. They received a federal contract to manufacture nine zeppelins for the military during World War I. The company also manufactured two airships for the military during the early 1930's, the *Akron* and the *Macon*. They had to build an enormous building to build the zeppelins. It's called the Goodyear Airdock and still stands today (pictured above).

At the ends of the building are identical semi-spherical doors, each weighing 600 tons. The doors are fastened at the top by hollow-forged pins, seventeen inches in diameter and six feet long. The doors rest on forty wheels set on curved railroad tracks.

During World War II, the company, then known as Goodyear Aircraft, manufactured airships for the military. It also built Corsair planes for the Navy. At this branch in 1939, they employed just thirty workers. With the outbreak of World War II, by 1942 the company consisted of thirty-five thousand employees. In just three years, that was an increase of 34,965 employees. The thousands of people who flocked to Akron had no problem finding employment.

The company now uses the ships almost exclusively for advertising purposes. In the 1950's the airships commonly appeared at major sporting events. The firm manufactured over three hundred zeppelins (more commonly called blimps) between 1917 and 1995, but it currently only operates four airships in the United States.

In 1963, the Goodyear Aircraft Corporation changed its name to the Goodyear Aerospace

Corporation. They played a major role in space exploration during the 1960's and the 1970's. They helped develop the heating and cooling systems for the Apollo spacecraft. In 1987, Goodyear sold the Aerospace plant to Loral. Now it is Lockheed Martin.

When my husband Duane and I lived on a point in the Portage Lakes we would often see the Goodyear blimp fly over, dipping lower to give the boaters a spectacular view. We could hear them approaching – the engine's sound is very distinguishable. I would always run out to watch when one flew over.

Occasionally, hot air balloons, in their beautifully bright colored patterns, would come over the lakes dipping low to just skim the surface of the water. I'm sure it was a challenge for them. I would think it would take a very skilled balloonist to pull that off. It would be so easy to miscalculate and end up taking an unexpected dip, which did happen once. The boater on the lake came to his rescue. One balloon had the name, Little Miss Muffet on the side.

Dad had four brothers that served in WWII. Bill and Rusty were in Europe, Floyd, a Seabee, and Bob were both in the navy in the Pacific arena. Dad was the oldest and the only one of the boys that was married during the war with one child. He thought he was going to miss being drafted, however, he finally got called in July of 1945 and arrived by train at the base when the announcement was made that the war was over. To start drafting family men tells one how bad the war situation was.

After leaving Goodyear, Dad pursued a business that eventually was very successful and would provide all his heart's desires – hunting and fishing trips, airplanes, a home in Canada, investment properties, and more. Unfortunately, there were disasters that lay ahead for him as well.

4

GOOD NEWS

I met my husband, Duane, on a double date. I was with the other guy and Duane was with the other girl. The guy I dated left soon after for the south without the intention of returning. One week after he left I received a call from you–know-who. He was known as "Mr. Personality" and he made quite an impression on me with his Irish traits – soft, blue eyes, pink skin and black wavy hair. I thought he was a very handsome man.

He was a tall and very confident man and no wonder; I found out later that he was a Staff Sergeant just out of the Marine Corps. I used to watch him as he talked to friends at church with his body language that was unlike any other. Yes, I was quite impressed, but never thought that we would be married some day.

We were married in 1958 but it wasn't until February 1970 that we learned at long last we were going to be a "family." Up until February of 1970 Duane and I had been married eleven years without children. We wanted to wait a few years, but not quite that long. We did consider adoption, but we were told we were too old. "Too Old!" I complained to Duane. "We're only thirty and thirty-seven. How can that be?" It seems the birth control pill, which was relatively new, was in high usage. It significantly reduced the availability of babies for adoption. In order to reduce the waiting list of prospective parents, the agencies set more restrictive qualifications. So with this pregnancy, we looked forward to all the exciting experiences that lay ahead of us. Our little one was due in October.

We enjoyed preparing the nursery for the baby, buying furniture, driving down to Millersburg, an Amish town, to buy a rocking chair at a small Amish store. Every mom has to have a rocker. Our son, his son and two girls were rocked in it and I expect our great grandchildren will all have the same experience. I find it gratifying to have something passed down in a family. Even though I don't have any furniture items from my ancestors I do have my grandfather's cane that he used most of his life and Duane has a flo-blue platter that his grandmother used on the ranch in the Nebraska Sand Hills outside of Ainsworth.

In August of 1970, I was seven months in my pregnancy when we decided to drive 1,200 miles to spend a few days with Dad in Gowganda. In the sixties he had built a nice two-bedroom cottage. It had a good sized kitchen and living room with the two rooms open to each other, making it look larger. And yes, there was indoor plumbing, so they did have a b-a-t-h r-o-o-m. Dad was such a very talented man with many abilities and could do most anything he pursued.

In my opinion there couldn't have been a better spot on the lake. It was on the north end with a wonderful, natural, sandy beach. Next to his cottage that he built, he and his neighbor bought the cabin on the west side and closer to the beach. This is where we always stayed. It had a wonderful view of Gowganda Lake through a picture window and sat directly behind that sandy beach.

I was looking forward to spending a few days with Dad at this special time in our lives. This was to be his first grandchild. I was thirty two and he was fifty one. He and mother were married at the young age of eighteen. I was hoping our visit would be an enjoyable one and it could be, if mother would exercise some control of her emotions. According to a psychiatrist she had a personality disorder. A social worker, who knew her well, said she had the traits of a sociopath. Our life (my dad, brother and I) with her was far more traumatic than tranquil and it did create many hurdles to overcome. But, worse than that, was the miserable life for her. She was trapped in a paranoid mind, never experiencing any release. From a very young age, I prayed for her ability to change.

When we first started going to The Chapel in Akron, the pastor was David Burnham. Many years ago he held a funeral for a member of the church who had committed suicide. Today, she probably would have been diagnosed as bipolar and could have been successfully treated. Dave said, "God knows the mind and He knows the heart and He knows the difference." I believe that for Mother.

On our visits to Canada, Mother started out well enough, but usually by the third day she could be screaming, usually accusing someone of stealing something. No one was ever surprised. It was expected; so we adjusted to the situation as best we could while trying to be as under- standing as possible. The definition of a sociopath can be very involved and complicated, but in short, a person with a personality disorder is known for antisocial behavior – a person who has little regard for the feelings of others and manipulates them in order to get what he/she desires. It's a description of an individual who has little to no sense of right versus wrong.

That, unfortunately, and sadly, describes my mother for the most part. She inflicted many deep wounds for both my brother and me. I survived through God's influence and love in my life. He also placed many wonderful caring people in my path including two surrogate mothers, Dee Powell and Hazel Suloff. Both have passed on and that has created a large void in my life. I miss them. *Thank you Hazel and Dee.*

Dad always tried his best to be certain we had an enjoyable visit by taking us fishing, going for drives, flying, or visiting friends. Another form of entertainment, believe it or not, was going to the dump to watch for bears and they were always there rummaging for food. One evening we were taking the trash to the dump and as Duane got to the edge of the dump to throw the bags over, he loudly cried, "There's a…b-b-b-bear!!!" That was the first time he saw one. We always enjoy teasing him about that.

GUY GATHERINGS

A large part of enjoying our stay, for me, was listening to the men who often came by to visit with

Dad and have a cold beer. He enjoyed the "Guy Gatherings." The cottage was a popular meeting place for his Canadian neighbors and the "Yankees," as we were often called. Dad loved to tell stories and could compete with the best of them. What is usually coupled along with that is not being a very good listener. I could always tell he couldn't wait until there was a gap in a conversation so he could jump in. Not to be out-shined, I suspect many of his stories could have been a wee bit embellished. He did like to keep a little levity in his conversations with his buddies. He enjoyed telling jokes. I can't remember most, but the ones I do remember, I had to include in his story:

> *When a man is losing his hair, there's a meaning as to how he is losing it. If it starts receding from the forehead it means he's a thinker. If it starts at the back of the head it means he is sexy. Now, if it starts at both places at the same time, it means he thinks he's sexy.*

Three skydivers asked a friend, Joe, who had never jumped in his life, to go out with them on a Saturday for a jump. Joe was reluctant, but not wanting to show his fear, he agreed. His friends said, "We'll give you all the instructions you'll need and at the end of the jump, there'll be a truck waiting for us." Well, after Joe jumped, his helmet flew off, his first parachute didn't open and the emergency one didn't open. "That's just great," Joe grumbled. "Now I suppose that stupid truck won't be there."

A guy took his blonde girlfriend to her first football game. They had great seats right behind their team's bench. After the game, he asked her how she liked it. "Oh, I really liked it," she replied, "especially the tight pants and all the big muscles, but I just couldn't understand why they were killing each other over twenty-five cents." Dumbfounded, her boyfriend asked, "What do you mean?" "Well, they flipped a coin, one team got it and then for the rest of the game, all they kept screaming was, 'Get the quarter back! Get the quarter back!' I'm like, Helloooooo. It's only 25 cents."

It was Dad's joke not mine.

As I sat in Dad's favorite old recliner he brought up from the States, listening quietly to m any of the gatherings, I thought it would be a great idea to record some of these lively and colorful conversations. However, I never did and of course, I have always regretted it. It would have been so much fun listening to them now.

The memories that I will never forget, however, are when he would take us flying in the 180 Cessna. In Akron, Ohio, where we lived, it was kept at the Fulton Airport most of the time. At one time, in the summer, it was kept on pontoons at Wingfoot Lake until Goodyear notified him he had to move out of that location. Goodyear wanted to create a park exclusively for their employees. They were thinking of the safety for the boaters. It is now open to the public so everyone can enjoy it.

When he flew to Gowganda, he would stop at the Orillia Airfield to remove the wheels and attach the pontoons. Then it was on to Gowganda. Landing in the lake, he could taxi right up to the dock in front of the cottage. That shoreline of the lake had that sandy beach I spoke of earlier, that gradually dropped off into pristine water.

What convenience and fulfillment that had to be for him as it represented dreams, planning, and many years of dedicated, hard work. He was not an idle person. There was always a project just ahead to be accomplished, a dream to be fulfilled. He had a strong philosophical work ethic plus the energetic drive to go with it. It would be remiss of me not to add, he was not a selfish person. He was always generous to others. That's how I like to remember the Gowganda Pilot.

5

GONE FISHING

Early on the morning of August 11,th I was awakened by the sound of Dad whistling while working in his garden outside. He was always an early riser and always whistled as he worked, whatever he was doing. He loved his life in Gowganda. Even now I can hear him whistling; what a good memory. I like to remember him that way as, The Whistling Pilot. Late on that afternoon Dad suggested we fly back in the "Bush" to fish. I was all for that because I loved fresh pickerel (south of the border they are called walleyes) dipped in beer batter and fried in an iron skillet like my mother prepared them. The fish were cleaned outside where Dad built a fish cleaning station. It kept the mess out of the kitchen and that just had to be Mother's idea.

About 4:30 p.m., we loaded up the plane with our fishing gear. Months before, Dad had removed the two back seats to make room for items such as fishing gear, a can of gas, emergency kit, floatation devices, etc. He kept an oar attached to the left pontoon. I always enjoyed the take-off; the force of water spraying back over the pontoons and the sound of the powerful engine as it picked up enough speed to lift off. It had to be up to fifty miles-per-hour for the lift off. That was always exciting to me. Boats on the lake would hurriedly scurry in every direction to get out of the way.

Dad was behind the controls; I was to his right in the front seat. Duane had to sit on the can of gas, which sounds very uncomfortable, but it was tolerable for a short flight. The flight took about twenty minutes by air. By land it would take at least three hours. Most of the lakes are not accessible by road so one has to portage to many of them, including the one we went to that day.

After landing at the lake, he eased the plane onto the only sandy spot of the lake. The rest of the shore was variable levels of very large rocks. We slowly worked the shoreline, climbing over the rocks as we went. Dad went to the left and Duane to the right. After about an hour of not having a single nibble, I decided that was enough for me, concluding it was going to be another fruitless flight. But that was alright. I enjoyed quite moments in the wilderness. I chose a smooth, flat rock, just the right height and sat down, laying my fishing rod beside me. I watched Dad as he would cast out and slowly reel in time after time without a single bite. He so wanted us to catch something and not go back empty handed. I could see there wasn't going to be any pickerel for dinner that night.

An interesting thing about Dad was that he loved to fish but, would not eat them – ever! I've always thought that was so unusual for such an avid fisherman. Often he would generously give the fish to others and of course, they would gladly accept them. As I sat there, my thoughts went back many years. Growing up before having an airplane, we spent time camping back in the "bush." That meant portaging over rough, woodsy terrain carrying a canoe, heavy camping equipment and being attacked by thousands of mosquitoes. They drove me crazy! Even heavily applied repellent didn't seem to help much. I was not a happy camper.

One time we camped on an island to avoid nosey bears. Well, that sounds good, but bears do know how to swim, and there was one on the island. Dad discovered it when he went into the woods to gather fire wood. He came back hollering to get the pots and pans. Mother turned so quickly, she sprained her ankle. We beat those pots so hard we made dents in them. It did scare the bear into the water and away from the island. We laughed about it later, but it wasn't so entertaining at the time.

Later, while setting up camp, Mother discovered that Dad had forgotten to pack the plates, which was his responsibility. "No problem," he said without concern. "We'll just tear some bark off the Birch trees."

"Gee, Dad, that sure sounds appetizing," I said somewhat sarcastically. So as we were flicking off a few insects and larvae, Dad said jokingly, "Leave them on, they're good protein." Obviously, he was a happy camper.

I refused to bathe in the lake. Just looking into the water I could see leeches on the bottom patiently waiting for one of us to jump in for their daily feast. Going a week without bathing or shampooing my hair, I was a mess. No, I was not a happy camper.

I will say this: those years spent camping and fishing in the wilderness did make a permanent, positive influence on me. They helped me develop toleration, patience, and a deep appreciation of comforts. I have never taken them for granted. I appreciate the beauty, scents, and sounds of forests and the creatures that inhabit them. I delight in pristine lakes and the fragrance in the air after a soft summer rain. I deeply appreciate the roof over my head and a soft bed in which to sleep. Every night when I go to bed I thank my Heavenly Father for these blessings.

Certain things don't bother me, such as a bug crawling on the table while dining outside, which brings a funny story to mind. I had invited two friends on a picnic. I provided the food and transportation. As we sat at a picnic table at Firestone Metropolitan Park eating our lunch, a bug landed on the box of chicken. Well, they went into a frenzy over that bug. You'd think it was a tarantula. I said, "Don't worry, he won't eat much."

They didn't laugh. I don't think they appreciated my sense of humor.

Firestone Metropolitan Park is one of Akron's many beautiful parks. It's situated a little southwest of the famous Firestone Golf Course where nationally televised golf tournaments are held every summer. One of the delights of Firestone Park is a certain area where one can walk holding out an upheld palm filled with sunflower seeds and sweet little Black-Capped Chickadees come from the trees and land on your hand. They are so light that you barely feel their little feet clutching your finger. On one occasion, one tried so hard, making several attempts to pick up two seeds at a time, but just couldn't handle it. Telling Dad about this unique little experience, he expressed that he would like to go there. I knew he would enjoy it and he did. I would love to be able to relive that moment.

6

THE PLUNGE

Dad broke my thoughts, announcing it was time to leave and we had stayed a little too long. The light was starting to fade and we needed to hurry back. Float planes like the Cessna are supposed to be down at light dusk. Unlike an airport there are no landing lights and a pilot can't see the water's surface in the dark.

I noticed how very still everything was – no air movement, not a flutter of leaves, no sound of birds…so very strange. I had never seen it like that. Everything reflected on the water without the least bit of distortion. It never occurred to me that such stillness could mean possible disaster. As we took off, just clearing the tree tops, I was thinking about Douglas, my eleven year old brother, who would be waiting at the dock for us. Whoever was at home had the responsibility of grabbing the strut and pulling the plane over to the dock and tying up. This was why Douglas would be waiting. As I was thinking about this, a thought flashed through my mind interrupting my thoughts……….PLANE CRASH!

I thought that was strange. I really didn't know what to make of it. Someone later suggested it was a natural reflex because I had a fear of flying but, I always enjoyed flying and never once, at any time, was fearful, so I couldn't accept that as an answer. In fact, the drone of the engine often lulled me to sleep. Flying in the Cessna was always an enjoyable experience. I ignored the thought and didn't think about it again. A few months later when telling our stories to friends, Duane said that at the very same time, just clearing the tree tops, he also had a premonition; however, his was visual, a newspaper article saying plane crash. He also ignored it.

Circling the lake and descending at the same time, we were about to touch down. I noticed the boats scurrying to get out of the way. I remember noting their boat lights were on, meaning it was dark enough for them to be on. It seemed like a normal landing to me. Landing on glassy water, I was told by experienced pilots later, is the most difficult landing to make because a pilot has no depth perception. The smooth surface acts like a mirror, reflecting everything up. The pilot has to watch the shoreline to estimate how close he is to the water.

I did notice that dad was glancing to his left, but he was lower than he realized, I have to assume, because the front tip of the left pontoon caught in the water sending the plane into cartwheels. All I could see was a gray blur spinning by the window. No one made a sound but, in my mind I was going, *OH! OH! OH!*

When the plane stopped, we were in an upside-down position. The windows popped out on impact causing the cabin to immediately fill with water. In my mind, I thought the plane was sinking down to the bottom of the lake which was about fifty feet deep. That was the worst part because it was a mental picture of a dark, inescapable pit and inexplicable horror.

I remember the haunting sounds of metal wrenching and the sound of water gushing through the windows filling the cockpit with water eliminating all pockets of air. It's difficult to recount those memories. I thought they were buried forever, never to surface again, at least not quite so vividly. For months after the accident I had repeating nightmares, waking, gasping for air. Opening my eyes, I couldn't see a thing, even though the water was pristine. It was now very dusk, dusk enough to turn the water dark. Like most people, I have a fear of deep, dark water.

I remember thinking, I'll not be able to get the door open, as it was always difficult for me to lock and unlock. Dad always had to assist me. It had a long track where the handle slid across locking the door. If I do get it unlocked, I thought, and push the door open, I won't be able to swim all the way up to the surface, still thinking we had settled on the bottom of the lake. In spite of all the negative factors I was somehow incredibly confident that I was going to survive…somehow.

One day in February of that year, I stood in our dining room and prayed to my Heavenly Father that He would grant us a son. We would bring him up according to His will and dedicate him back to His service, whatever that would be. Unknowingly at the time, this was just like Hanna's prayer in the Old Testament. Assuredly, I told myself trapped in that plane and drowning, I know I am supposed to have this baby because he was an answer to my prayer.

I was trying to breathe, but with each attempt I was taking in water. So, this is how one drowns, I thought…it's suffocation. It was terrifying not being able to take in oxygen. It's something most all of us take for granted. I was hanging upside down and with great effort I had to pull myself up to find the seat buckle to release it. I was seven months pregnant and this was very difficult, pregnant or not. Strangely enough, I never once panicked. My thoughts were logical and focused on what I needed to do.

Straining to pull myself up the second time, I still didn't find the buckle. Consciously I moved my hand around my lap, still inhaling water...no buckle. Each time, pulling up became more and more difficult. Falling back the second time, my thoughts began to change; perhaps there is to be no escape for me. I'll just relax and accept the consequences, as difficult as they will be.

However, for some reason I cannot explain, I was motivated to try one more time. Maybe subconsciously I couldn't accept defeat. I don't know for certain, but I like to think it was God's Spirit urging me to try one more time because this time I was not thinking about where my hands were going. They automatically went under my left leg and there it was. Thank you, Father. What a relief. But, I knew my struggle wasn't over yet. Having finally released the buckle I turned to open the door thinking, even if I do get this door open, I won't be able to swim all the way to the surface. I've taken In so much water I won't have that much time left. Great was my surprise when I immediately rolled out of the plane. I quickly started to the surface.

7

RESCUED

Immediately breaking the surface, to my surprise, I saw the pontoons on top of the water which kept the plane afloat. How wonderful! I hadn't thought of that and no wonder, since I was kept so busy struggling to get out. But now I was alone and it was so still and quiet. My elation of surviving and being able to take in deep, deep breaths of wonderful life-sustaining oxygen quickly turned to dread. Thoughts formed in my mind of them being trapped, injured, or worse.

Taking a deep breath I prepared to go back down for them, not knowing what I could or would do, but I had to do something. As I started to go under, Duane's head popped up, gasping for air. He looked over at me saying, "Oh, am I ever glad to see you." Then Dad came up gasping and coughing – extremely distraught. I could see he was in a far worse state than Duane or me. I wondered why? He kept saying, "I couldn't get it open. I couldn't get it open." He was so upset that I was very concerned for him. Later, I was to learn his version of what happened.

As they pulled themselves up onto the pontoons, they were asking me, with much concern, if I was alright. I assured them I was fine. My concern was for them and I asked, "Are you alright?" "Yes," was their reply. They carefully pulled me up onto the pontoons. As I steadied myself on top I observed that it was dark enough that I couldn't see any boats approaching to help. Surely they saw what happened. So I said, "Let's all yell 'help' at the same time. One, two, three......HELP! HELP!"

Yelling wasn't necessary – boats were on the way, but we just couldn't see them. Soon a white shirt started appearing through the darkness and the closer it came I knew it had to be Burt Somerville, Dad's Canadian next door neighbor. He always wore white tee-shirts in the summer. I calmly called out to him, "Burt, is that you?" "Aye," he responded. "I ran to my boot to get out here as fast as I could." Many Canadians pronounce boat as boot. I love it. Burt and his wife, Ruthie, lived in Gowganda year-round. He was such a likeable person…could talk like an old salt at times, but we overlooked that because of his goodness and sense of humor. His appearance reminded me a little of a mature Paul Newman. He would do so many thoughtful favors for Dad, such as preparing Dad's garden before he came up in the spring or mowing the grass. After Dad retired at the age of fifty, he usually went up in May and back to the States in September. During his summer stay he made certain to repay Burt in various ways. Burt was an interesting character. I loved to listen to him talk and tell his humorous stories that were plentiful. I miss him and his wonderful sense of humor.

Dad loved gardening, flowers, and vegetables. When he put in the veggie garden he wanted the very best kind of soil, so he brought in railroad ties and built a raised garden, two ties high, in order to create the soil he wanted. It was a mixture of sand, peat moss, top soil, and dehydrated cow manure. It was wonderful and oh my, how those veggies thrived. When we visited in the summer, Dad and I would work in that garden together sometimes weeding or pulling onions, plucking sweet peas off the vine and popping them into our mouth. Those are some of the best memories for me.

Dad's favorite flower was hybrid oriental lilies because of their outstanding beauty and their most delightful, sweet fragrance. He had clusters of them of various colors lining the stone walk approaching the door of the cottage. I'm certain that's why I had so many in my English garden at our home in Portage Lakes south of Akron. The lilies drew so many beautiful, entertaining humming birds. Once, one caught its bill in the screen door. Dad picked up a pencil and with the erasure end, gently pushed the bird's bill back through the screen. Uninjured, it flew away to gather more nectar from the lilies. I was so impressed with his ingenuity and gentleness. I don't think I had ever seen him quite that way before. One exception would be when I was seven I had stubbed my toe and hearing my pain he bent down and held my foot in his hand saying gently, "Oh, I know how that hurts." That surprised me even then because I had not heard such gentleness from him.

Dad was not one to show a soft side. When it came to showing affection like giving me a hug, he would stiffen with his arms tight to his sides and could not or would not reciprocate. Once, when giving him a hug, with his right hand he gave me a quick pat on my shoulder. That was it. He was just one of those people that have difficulty displaying affection.

Burt pulled up beside the pontoons and Dad and Duane started for his boat. Duane, turning to me, commanded, "Come on." I tried, but could not move my legs, as hard as I tried, they just would not move. "I can't move my legs," I cried back. It was the first moment that I realized that I had sustained some kind of injury. After they helped me into the boat, which was not easy because I was like a heavy bag of wet sand, Burt sped towards the cottage on the north shore. I could see the amber glow of the cottage lights along the north shoreline that seemed like welcoming beacons...a glorious, comforting sight.

On the way, I remembered Douglas. He had to have witnessed the accident as he was supposed to be at the dock waiting to help dock the plane. Later I learned that he did see it and ran stumbling and screaming to the cottage to tell Mother. Burt, working outside, hearing Douglas, knew what had happened and hurried to his boat. He had to have had that motor at top speed, because he arrived sooner than the boats which were already on the lake. Many years later, Doug said he remembers the sight and sound of the prop hitting the water and seeing the red lights sinking into the water. What a terrifying experience for him.

8

GOING ASHORE

As we approached the dock, I could see a large number of cars parked around the cottage. It seems we were quite an attraction. Some were caring neighbors who came to offer assistance in any way they could. Others were there out of curiosity. I'm sure word of the crash spread like a prairie fire.

Duane and Dad carried me through the people who had gathered outside and into the cottage, carefully laying me on the sofa. The room was filled with people. I don't remember who they were because I was preoccupied with myself due to the pain I was now experiencing that could not be ignored. I had never experienced anything like it, nor do I ever want to again.

I looked at my shirt which was ripped and, of course, my clothes were soaking wet. My long hair that was pulled up was now hanging down over my face. I tried to brush it back when pain shot through my arms. I didn't dare try to move my legs as the pain was unbearable. I glanced up at the window and saw curious faces of children peering in. I wonder what they must have thought. I had to have been quite a spectacle to them. Duane and Dad were becoming ill as shock started to set in. I wasn't experiencing shock symptoms and thank God for that. My body was experiencing too much as it was plus, shock would be dangerous to the baby.

Burt and some neighbors were filling his station wagon with sleeping bags to provide a soft ride to the hospital. I was told Cathie White was one of those helping. She and her husband owned the lodge and cabins across the bay. Cathie told me recently that years ago she had asked Dad, "How did you do it!" Dad said simply, "I had to!" *Thanks to all who helped that evening.*

The nearest hospital, I was told, was at Englehart, fifty miles away. That was to be a very arduous and painful journey. The dirt road out of Gowganda was rough and winding with some stretches over bed rock. Burt drove as carefully as he could, but every time the wagon hit a bump or made a turn, I screamed out, unable to contain it. Burt must have felt badly, but it couldn't be helped. I just had to bite the bullet and too bad there wasn't one around – I could have used a box of them. Burt gave so much of himself that day. *Thank you Burt.*

During the drive, Dad, in his ill state, explained what he meant when he said, "I couldn't get it open." It seems that while I was trapped and struggling to open the seat belt, he was kicking across me to kick my door open. He said that he kicked over and over again. He didn't realize how successful he was in the process of allowing us to escape. I told him that he was responsible for saving four lives: his own,

Duane's, mine, and David, our unborn son. Later, we found out after the plane was towed back to shore and up-righted that he had not only kicked the door open, but in fact, kicked the door entirely off the hinges and it was at the bottom of the lake and remains there to this day. I was told by a pilot later in time that it would be extremely difficult to kick off the door because of the way the planes are constructed, and under water would have to be even more difficult. No wonder Dad was in such an emotional and physical state after he surfaced. He had made a frantic, ultimate effort to save our lives. *Thank you ten thousand times, Dad.*

My brother told me something recently that I had not known all these years. I had always assumed that Dad went out his door, but apparently he couldn't get his open far enough to get through it. The flap on the left wing was bent down preventing his door to fully open. He exited through the opening he created when he kicked off my door. He couldn't exit until I did. Now the picture was clear to me. If he had been unsuccessful in kicking open my door, we would have all drowned. I shudder when I think of how very close we came to being fatalities that day. It greatly amplifies the strength and determination of his efforts.

Duane, who was sitting on the can of gas, was tossed around in the plane and was dazed; however, he did quickly catch a breath of air from an air pocket before it quickly vanished. All he remembers is clawing at the side of the windows and feeling a hand that he couldn't see reaching back for him. He followed that hand and squeezed through Dad's door, pushing hard to open it wider.

9

AT THE HOSPITAL

After what seemed an eternity, we finally arrived at the Englehart hospital. By this time I was starting to have contractions which understandably concerned me, while at the same time I was grateful to be at the hospital. I was put in the maternity ward in the event that I would go into labor. The doctor immediately gave me a shot of some kind of pain killer. I don't know what it was, but it was very effective as all my pain immediately left and what a wonderful relief that was. The doctor also gave Dad and Duane something for their sickness.

The next day, after the pain returned, I asked if I could please have another shot like the night before. I was given just one more and was told they couldn't give any more because of the possibility of endangering the wellness of the baby. I understood and went back to biting the bullet. I told myself that nothing in the future could be as bad as what I was experiencing then, so the worst was going to be behind me. So far that has been true.

The weather was unusually hot and humid, in the nineties, which is a rare thing. The hospital didn't have central air because they really didn't need it before. The heat made it very uncomfortable, so much so that Duane went into town to different stores trying to find an electric fan for me, but without success. Somehow, a patient in the hospital heard about me and gave her fan to a nurse with instructions to give it to me. What a thoughtful and sacrificing lady. I wish I could have personally thanked that patient.

How many people would have done that? *A much belated thank you to that lady.*

The next day I was unable to move a solitary muscle. It felt like every muscle in my body was strained. I also noticed how badly bruised I was.... from head to toe. I didn't realize I was so violently knocked around. It made me wonder. Most likely, Dad was not always hitting his target – the door. He had to also be kicking me since I was between him and my door. I never mentioned that to him; however he may have thought of it himself.

Mother had to spoon feed me for two days as I couldn't lift my head or arms. My pelvis and legs were the most painful areas. At the time, no one knew the extent of my injuries. The doctor explained that x-rays could not be taken out of concern for the baby.

Sometime after David was born, I did go to an orthopedic doctor to find out if anything would still show up on x-ray. I was curious as to what actually did happen, plus I was asked to speak at a ladies group at church about the accident and wanted to report the story accurately. The results were: a fractured pelvis in two places, the coccyx (tail bone) was completely snapped off and was now a floater somewhere in the abdominal area, thigh muscles were torn on the right leg, and muscles that cross the back of the pelvis were "pulverized" as the doctor put it. My theme for the presentation to the ladies group was: "Good things can come out of every crisis."

Back at Gowganda the morning after the crash, Burt went out to where the plane was still floating in the water and took a shot of it. The picture shows only the pontoons on top of the water. The plane was totally submerged. Looking at the picture, it doesn't look so serious, but being trapped inside could make it lethal – and it almost was. I still shudder when I look at that picture.

With a tow line attached, it was towed back and turned right-side up on the public beach. The picture doesn't show the front and right side, which is where most of the damage was done. Some of the residents and visitors came to watch and inspect the damage. As far as I know, historically, it was the only plane crash on the lake. I hope that's true. In a previous visit to Gowganda, there had been an accident up at the silver mine. As I recall, I think the pilot got out without injuries. We were thankful for that. We drove up to see the plane. It didn't look too badly damaged because he aimed for the road that led through the camp. His plane was on wheels, not pontoons. Apparently he was lost and ran out of gas. Planes like the Cessna have a high gliding ratio depending on the altitude. If the pilot is flying at 5,000 feet, a common height, and the engine stalls, it can glide approximately five miles. Within that range, there is bound to be a lake since there are so many in that territory providing a pilot several landing options. Having wheels on a plane in that territory is not a good idea.

Duane and Dad were at the cottage most of the time recovering from their shock. The medication the doctor gave them did help them from feeling much worse. Dad had somehow scraped the top of his head….badly enough for the doctor to treat it so it would heal properly. Eighteen years later he would have a much more serious head trauma which was to be another brush with death with a miraculous survival, but it had long-term consequences.

On the third day after the crash, Duane drove to the hospital to talk with the doctor about an early release. I had no knowledge of this conversation. I was still in intense pain and having contractions. If someone had asked me if I wanted to go home early, I would have emphatically said it was too soon. Unfortunately, no one asked for my opinion. The doctor told Duane it was too early, but he eventually caved in to Duane's perseverance on the matter.

10

BACK TO THE COTTAGE

By the third day I could move a little better (very little) but the pain was just as unbearable and would remain so for another couple of months. I found out that I was going back to the cottage that day. Duane and Dad were outside waiting to take me back to Gowganda. Dad whistled and sang all the way. He was the happy whistler once again. The song he sang was:

> Many things about tomorrow I don't
> seem to understand,

But, I know who holds the future and I know who holds my hand.

When we arrived at the cottage, friends were there to welcome me back. They didn't stay long though, out of consideration for me. Mother was waiting with her camera and took a shot of us on our arrival. I tried taking a nap, but just couldn't find a comfortable position without experiencing pain. What did work fairly well was Dad's old recliner from the States.

Burt came over for a brief visit which gave me the opportunity to thank him for all he did. I wanted to convey the extent of our gratitude. He commented on how surprised he was when he heard my calm voice calling out to him when he arrived at the plane that night. Maybe he expected us, or me, to be panic stricken. He did say that on the way out he thought he would be diving down to pull us out. What a remarkable person.

An Ontario Provincial Policeman, OPP (comparable to our State Highway Patrol) came into

Gowganda to fill out a report on what happened. Dad was certain he had hit something that was in the water. When the policeman turned to me asking, "What is your account of what happened?" I couldn't say we hit something other than the water, and yet I didn't want to say something that would contradict Dad, so I just said, "All I know is we hit hard." He later filled out his report as pilot error. Some of the people that witnessed the crash were interviewed by the policeman and their statements were that the plane was too low.

But, there is another story to this. Something I recently learned from my brother that I did not know was this: Dad did some investigating of his own and he learned that the company that made the pontoons had gone out of business due to law suits against them. Apparently, the law suits were the result of accidents just like Dad's. He found out the pontoons were the cause of the accidents due to a bad design on the front end that could cause them to dig in. I don't know the technical details.

Dad and Duane drove me down to see the plane which was still on the public beach. I could see that the right door was gone, hinges and all; the pontoons were bent, the prop was mostly gone, all the skin of the plane was wrenched and, of course, the windows were gone. "That's enough." I said. "Let's go back to the cottage." It was a good thing that Douglas didn't go that day. He was supposed to, but didn't because of a bad cold.

It is interesting to note that Dad and Duane went into a semi-mild state of shock, but I didn't. I remained very buoyed in spirit. Everyone marveled at this. "How is it that you're so uplifted after what you've been through?" some would ask. At that time I couldn't give them an answer other than, "It's just so great to be alive."

After I got back to my doctor in Akron, he told me that if I had gone into shock, Duane would have lost both of us. There was my answer. God's Spirit kept me buoyed to protect me and the baby. *Thank you Heavenly Father for your saving presence.*

Back at the cottage, Dad and I started recounting some of the events when I was growing up. He taught me how to fish, how to make flies for fly casting, use the bow and arrow, how to fire a rifle, how to pitch a soft ball, and more. We would occasionally go to a rifle range and target practice. When I was ten, he made a .22 rifle of curly maple and inset pearl diamonds in the stock. This was a present to me. He obviously spent a great deal of time on it and even though I wasn't big on rifles, I did value that one.

Duane and I had been married about nine years when Dad bought us two Ethica shot guns for Christmas. Duane's parents had a farm in Rootstown where we could skeet shoot. A shot gun isn't something that holds first place for a gift, but I accepted it graciously.

Sometime later, our house was burglarized and many items were stolen including the two beautiful shotguns and the 22 rifle he made for me. Dad was miffed about that. He didn't say so, but I got the impression that he thought we were careless in some way, but we had locked the house. That, obviously, didn't stop the burglars. The guns expressed how he wanted us to have something that he thought was a valuable gift. I felt very badly about losing them. I suspect Dad probably, subconsciously, or maybe consciously, wanted me to be a boy. He certainly tried his best to make me a tomboy.

One additional way was going out to pitch some balls after coming home from work. "Go get your mitt and let's pitch a few," he would say. He pitched and I caught. He didn't go easy on me either. His fast pitches stung as they slammed into my mitt causing me to cry out, "Ow!" He claimed it would toughen me up. Uh-huh.

I received the mitt and a softball as a Christmas present – just what a girl dreams about. He loved baseball. When he lived in Springfield, where I was born, he was the pitcher for the Ohio Edison Baseball team. When pitching to me I had to remind him I was not their catcher.

When Dad applied for a job at Ohio Edison he met Bob Miller who hired him in spite of being under age. Dad wasn't quite eighteen, but apparently Bob took a liking to Dad, perhaps seeing the potential in him. Dad was always grateful to Bob and maintained their friendship for many years even after moving to Akron.

11

BREAK DOWN

The first night back at the cottage was not good. There was no sleep and not a moment's relief from the tormenting pain. I wondered why the doctor didn't give me pain medication to help in the days ahead. That would have made a huge difference. Duane tried to help, but I was inconsolable.

Very early the next morning, Duane announced he was leaving to go back to the States and I was to stay there. That came as a complete surprise. I was stunned. My response was, "You're leaving? Why can't I go with you?" "Those were the terms the doctor set," he said. "You can't go back yet. Can't you stay with me a little longer?" "No, I have to get back to work. As soon as I'm packed, I'm taking off."

At that stage of my life I hadn't discovered my voice. If I had the stronger voice I found in my forties, I would have presented a much stronger case for myself. At the right time, in the right situation, women need to express their opinions. God doesn't frown on that if it is done unselfishly, thoughtfully, and in the right way. Men usually don't know what is on our minds unless we tell them. It has to be done calmly, without emotion, and in a logical and practical way. Possibly, it might be needed to be done a little differently with different men. My husband was accustomed to attending board meetings at the bank. So, I presented everything as though I was sitting in that board meeting. When I did this, he would lend me his ears and mind. I can't remember a single time when this technique did not work.

Weeks later, when touching on the subject of him leaving, he told me he thought I would be alright since I enjoyed being with my Dad and it seemed I was doing so well. "SO WELL!" I thought. How could he be so dead wrong? I was astonished at his answer, but giving it a lot of thought, I suppose that everyone thought I was doing well because my spirits were high in spite of the severe pain I was experiencing, plus the contractions. Apparently, no one knew just how badly I was suffering. Maybe I should have been more vocal about it and I guess I was too good at biting that bullet.

It was important to Duane to return to work as scheduled. That's why he talked the doctor into letting me go early. He didn't want to leave for home with me still in the hospital and for a while I truly thought I could handle staying without him, but the mood completely changed when he left and the reality of his absence and my situation set in like a ton of wet sand falling on me. I felt alone and very, very frightened.

Still having contractions, I wanted to feel the safety of being home and seeing my doctor. I felt the urgency of making that happen. It was too risky to stay and I knew it. The big question was, did everyone else know it...I didn't think so. I was afraid of going into labor and losing the baby and being sixty miles from the Englehart hospital was not the least bit calming. With Duane not being there with me, I'm embarrassed to say, I lost all composure. The full impact of what had happened caused the flood gates to burst. All the emotions came pouring out. I was surprised at the drastic emotional change that took place, from being so serene to dissolving into uncontrollable sobbing. It was so traumatic.

I was with Mother in the bedroom and asked if she could call ahead to Elk Lake where a friend lived. Perhaps he could flag Duane down as he went through town, asking him to return. However, that didn't work as he had already driven past the town. Now I knew it was hopeless. Dad was in the living room and, hearing the commotion, he came bursting into the bedroom, slamming door against the wall. His demeanor told me he was upset and when he opened his mouth, I knew he was very upset. "You're acting like a baby," he shouted, his face distorted and red with anger. Obviously, this upset me even more and was not what I needed.

I turned away from him not able to look at him like that. He had never, ever turned that side of himself to me. I thought he would be more understanding. He could have helped the situation by bringing it under control with a soft, calming, thoughtful voice, assuring me that everything was going to be alright and I believe that would have been quite effective. Unfortunately, he was not accustomed to responding in this manner. He expected me to suck-it-up at his command. He was playing Mr. Tough Guy.

My response to him could have been: "This is, hopefully, to be your first grandchild. Duane isn't here. We've waited eleven years. I'm in tremendous pain. I haven't slept in three days. I'm having contractions. I'm 1,200 miles from my doctor. I don't know if I will miscarry or not. I think those are valid reasons for being upset." But, I didn't. I just whined, "I want to go home."

Perhaps he didn't like how I was carrying on, maybe he really wanted me to stay, or maybe he didn't want Mother to drive me all the way home... that's what she was planning. I don't know. That event never came up for discussion and I believe it was best forgotten.

Dad and one of his Cessnas

Davey at the cottage 1971

First Christmas

Our first Christmas after the crash

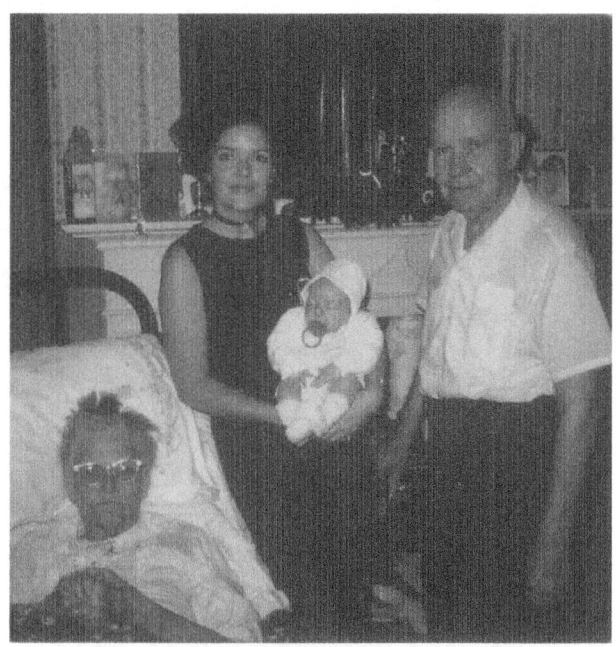

First Christmas with Pop and Mattie
3 months after the crash

David on his Grampa Craig's farm

1948 Hunting trip to Wyoming
Dad in the middle

Pat, Burt and Dad

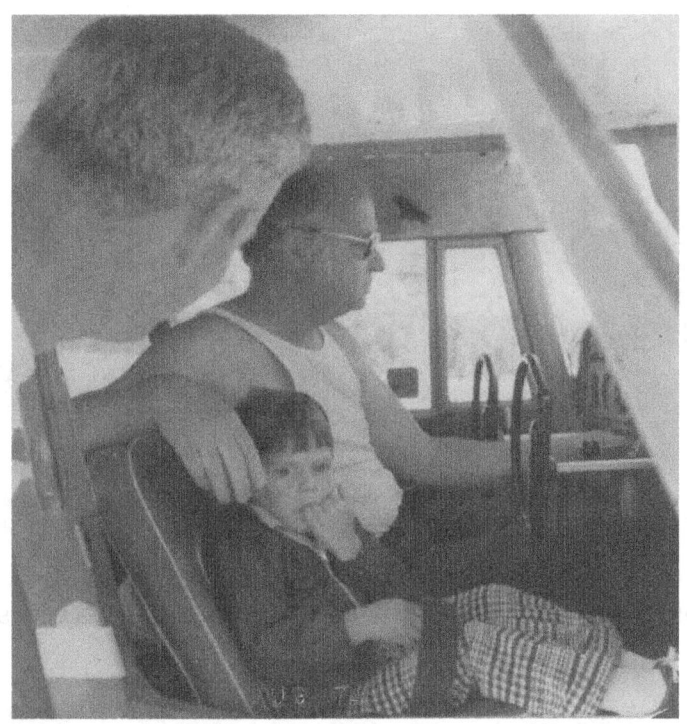

David's first plane ride with Burt in the foreground

Cessna in flight

Air hangar with Mrs. Litchfield and some banker's wives

K-3 Blimp 1477

The "SeaBee," Dad's first plane

Macon in the Goodyear Air Dock 1933

Patsy

Baby Jerry

Me and Dad's 1936 Ford

Dad and me in Jackson,

Mother at age 18

Dad's brother Floyd, the SeaBee, Served in WWII

Dad's brother Bob Served in WWII

Bob, far left somewhere in the South Pacific

The morning after the crash

Plane uprighted on shore

Coming back to the cottage from Englehart Hospital

Dad's cottage

View from the cottage

Ohio Edison baseball team in Springfield, Ohio. Dad in the middle row. Taken about 1937

Dad and me in 1949

Great Uncle Ralph's farm

Duane at Cherry Point

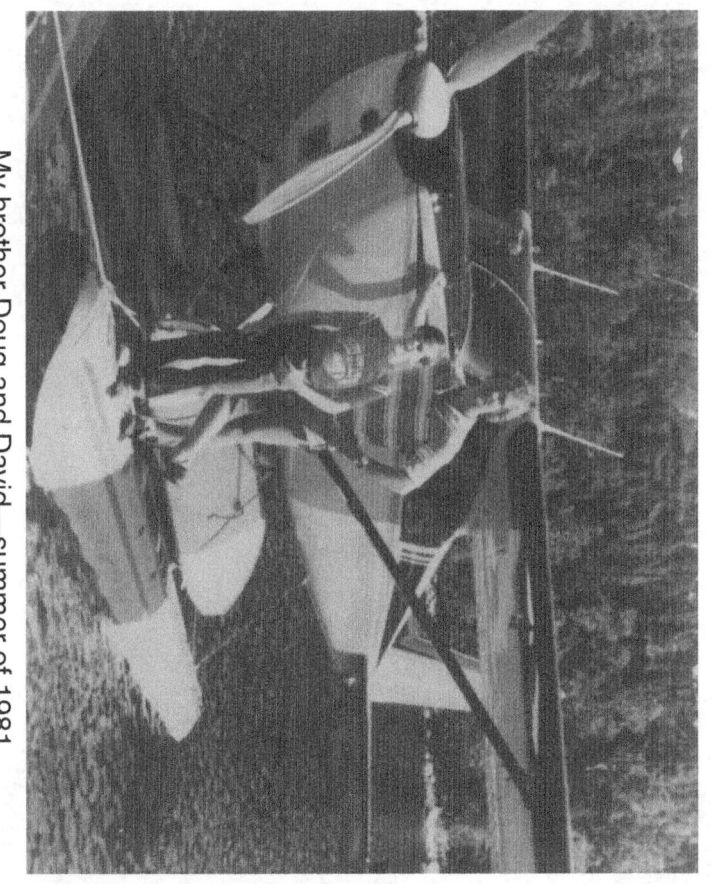

My brother Doug and David—summer of 1981

Proud Dave with pike catch

Dad with Dad

My brother Doug and me

David and Angie, Abby, Drew, Ashlyn

Harvey and Marjanna Craig, 2nd generation on farm

The Craig farm in Rootstown, Ohio

Duane's father Delbert and our son David on the Ford Ferguson

David feeding Grampa's White Face cows

12

THE LONG TRIP HOME

Early the next morning Mother and I packed, preparing for the long trip home. She had to help me with my packing as I was unable to handle much of it. Looking ahead, I dreaded the two days it would take to get back. The trip would be difficult for me and for her and I felt badly about that as I was the cause of her having to drive me back to Ohio. However, the right decision was made. I had to get back. We noticed that Dad wasn't around and suspected he was avoiding us by pretending to be busy with some needless chore outside.

When we were ready to leave, I thought I would see him come around the cottage approaching the station wagon to say goodbye. He didn't. I wondered if it was too difficult for him to say goodbye and wish us a safe trip back to the States. He had his reasons I suppose; maybe his anger hadn't subsided enough or maybe it was just stubbornness. That's possible. Maybe it was just too difficult for him to say goodbye. That's what I chose to believe. I would have liked to have given him a hug before leaving and hind sight tells me that I should have gone to him and given him a loving hug, wanting it or not. Having said before that he was not a person who could show affection, I knew he did care. He showed it in different ways.

Some of that trait could have come from his mother, Mattie. She was a very unemotional person except for crankiness. Come to think of it, I was never on the receiving end of any display of affection from her, verbally or physically. Her only daughter, Joanne, once told me about a conversation between them. When asking her mother, "Why is it you never compliment me on how I look or how well I'm doing in school? You never say anything complimentary to me." Mattie quickly snapped back, "When you do something bad, I'll let you know. Otherwise you're ok." How about that for motherly love? I find it sad that people can go through life never experiencing some of the most precious and fulfilling experiences in life. They willingly deny themselves those blessings and it doesn't have to be that way. God's love is available to everyone.

My grandfather was the opposite of Mattie. He was a wonderful, sweet-spirited man and a huge influence on me as a child. He was not successful or wealthy as the world measures it. He was wealthy in other ways that count for eternity. He told me once that when someone wants to give us something or do something for us, we should not refuse that gift because it will deny that person of a blessing. Dad worked long hours in his business and was not always available to take me different places such as school activities, girl scout camp, etc. He would ask my grandfather (Pop) to take me and of course, Pop was always more than willing. When I was in first grade a girl in my class, Gaye Kaiser, ran into the street from between two parked cars and was struck by a car and killed. Pop took me to that funeral. I thought at the time that it was strange; I didn't ask to go, but I went. I suspect Dad thought it would be a good experience to teach me a lesson and it did – I never forgot.

Another lesson he taught me was when I received my first speeding ticket at eighteen. (My first and only I should add.) We had moved from the old neighborhood into a new one much farther from my high school. He provided me with a one year old, red and white 1956 Oldsmobile for transportation. It was beautiful and flashy. Running a little late for school one day, I exceeded the speed limit…a little. The first words I heard the patrolman say were, "Good morning, beautiful day isn't it?" I don't think too many people hear that when stopped for speeding. He must have recently had a lesson on public relations. Anyway, I thought it was much nicer than getting a scolding, which probably would have been appropriate. When Dad found out, he obviously was upset. "You'll go with me won't you?" "No," was his response. "You got the ticket, you take the punishment." And so I did. The judge presiding in traffic court that day was Judge Zook. I can't believe I remember his name. He was not very pleasant either.

It's most interesting how that car made me instantly popular at school. There was only one other student that drove a car to school, unlike now. Now half the cars in the parking lot belong to students. I was the talk of the school… Pat had that flashy red and white Oldsmobile. The more forward classmates would quickly approach me at the sound of the lunch bell saying, "Hey, Pat, let's hop in your car and go to the B&K for lunch." And so we did. That was in 1957 and incredibly, that stand is still there. The last time I was by it was in 2011 and it was still there. I could see that red and white Oldsmobile sitting there with a tray braced on the driver's window filled with frosted mugs of cold root beer.

Many times Pop would pick me up on Sunday mornings to take me to his church. He loved to sing the old hymns and quickly responded if asked to sing. Using his cane he would climb the three steps up on the stage and sing with great gusto, belting out those songs. He loved it. I remember, "The Preacher and the Bear," "Heavenly Sunshine," "How I Love Jesus." These were a few of his favorites.

Heading south on the QUE, (Queen Elizabeth Highway) my thoughts finally turned to what lay ahead: calling the doctor to set an appointment; what to tell Duane; how to explain what happened; being embarrassed if I did; what to do about meals; how would I manage when Duane was at the bank all day? I tried to ease and calm my mind by telling myself, "I have to take this one day, one thing, at a time."

The time to drive from Gowganda to Akron was approximately thirteen hours. Duane and I always divided the time into two days. Dad on the other hand never did. He seemed to take pride, for some reason known only to him, in driving it in one day. The insane thing was, he was always trying to break his record, boasting when he arrived at his destination, going north or going south, that he knocked off another ten or fifteen minutes. When he drove, it was because he was between airplanes. One could accurately say he liked to "fly low." These same kinds of circumstances would bring about a devastating tragedy nineteen years later.

Mother drove all the way, occasionally stopping at a parking lot to nap. That trip to get me home was no small effort on her part. She clearly sensed the emotional and physical importance of it. When we needed to eat, she would usually bring something to the car. When I had to walk it was done s-o-o-o-o slowly. If someone saw us, they would wonder what was going on. Placing one foot out at a time was impossible because it meant I had to use the thigh muscle. I had to wear socks and advance my feet by crunching up my toes moving them forward. It's difficult to describe. It took me forever to get to my destination, praying as I went that I would get to the restroom in time.

13

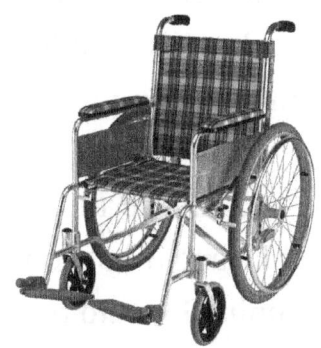

HOME AT LAST

Once I arrived home, I immediately called my doctor. I don't know what made me think I was going to get in right away. Telling the receptionist I was in a plane crash didn't seem to be urgent enough to squeeze me in. I was told they couldn't work me in for another five days. I was on the sofa night and day. When Duane left for work, I was on the sofa and when he came home from work, I was on the sofa. The first day I called a friend and neighbor asking if she would be so kind to make a lunch for me and of course, she willingly prepared a very nice lunch for me. I was grateful. She offered to bring another the next day, but not wanting to impose on her again, I said I would be alright. I probably should have allowed her to do that. I did need someone during the day. My grandfather would have said I denied her that blessing.

Being on the sofa all the time, I became quite depressed. I asked Duane if he would rent a wheelchair for me, explaining I would be in a much better frame of mind if I could move around the house. Mother took me to the doctor's appointment allowing an extra thirty minutes to make my snail-pace, toe-crunching entrance. I told the doctor about what had happened and that I hadn't slept in five days and was still in immense pain. As I mentioned before, he said that if I had gone into shock, Duane would have lost both of us. This is one of the many ways that I know our Heavenly Father cares for us.

Upon taking a blood sample, I was told my blood count was extremely low. This was the result of the trauma, pain, and lack of sleep. He gave me a prescription for a mild codeine for the pain and something to help me sleep. It was wonderful to get relief from the pain and the ability to sleep, sleep, sleep.

When I got back from the doctor's office I found the wheel chair that Duane had brought home and once I had the opportunity to use it, it did indeed make a world of difference. My spirits were lifted 100%. Rolling it to the front of the kitchen sink, I could stand up to do the dishes. I just couldn't move my legs. I remember how the bubbles from the dish detergent floated in the air, reflecting beautiful colors of the rainbow. I took delight in that. How pleasing it is to appreciate such little things. Duane and I both were given a greater appreciation of everything. You could say we were on cloud nine. Between the medication, sleep, and the wheelchair I was starting to feel much better physically and emotionally. My life was slowly getting back to normal.

By the time David was born, October 26th 1970, my injuries had mostly healed; there was just a slight limp of my right leg. Gratefulness filled my heart. Mother spent time at the house helping with the needs of a newborn baby. I appreciated her being there and it was encouraging to see her in a good frame of mind. I was hopeful it would be an indication of future stability for her. *Thank you Mother.*

UNCLE RALPH AND AUNT RUTH

When Mother was in her twenties and thirties, she would disappear for two to three weeks without telling anyone where she was going or how long. When returning, she never told anyone where she had gone. I suspect though, she went to visit her sister Billy. Billy was like a mother figure to her. When I was four, Mother was gone the entire summer and Dad had to find someone to take care of me. He decided to take me to his uncle's farm in Beaver, Ohio. He was Mattie's brother, Ralph Kern and his wife was Ruth. They were kind enough to take me in for the summer or until Mother returned. It was an easy role for them as I was not a problem child. I enjoyed pleasing people and I actually enjoyed my summer with them. I don't remember missing Mother at all. I was accustomed to entertaining myself. Ralph's farm had a shallow creek running along the road and I enjoyed wading in it. Occasionally I would see a crayfish that would make me scream like a typical little girl.

Uncle Ralph built their home himself as he was a carpenter and at one time had an accident while operating an electric saw and cut off part of two fingers on his right hand. He used to tease me and say, "If you don't behave yourself, I'll come after you with this stubby hand." It didn't really frighten me. I knew he was teasing. The house was made of yellow glazed blocks and had a front porch that went across the entire front of the house.

The drive was horse shoe shaped and crossed a wood bridge on each side crossing the creek. There was no plumbing for a bathroom so there was a privy behind the house. Chamber pots were provided in each of the four bedrooms. There was also a large pile of coal in the back yard for their coal burning stoves in the house used for cooking and heating. I remember studying the rainbows of color in the coal.

There was no electricity at the time. At night, I remember them carrying the oil lamp up the stairs, lighting the way ahead as darkness followed behind. Every night they would kneel by their bed with the feather stuffed mattress and pray aloud. That was the first time I ever heard someone pray. It made quite a lasting impression on me, much more than the quill ends of the feathers that poked through the sheets.

Their living room had a pot belly stove in the middle and I remember Ralph and I eating tangerines one day. They had an old grandfather's clock and being in the country side it was so very quiet. All you could hear was the pendulum of that old clock. Tick....Tick.....Tick....Tick. Aunt Ruth cooked on a large iron wood-burning stove. It had a trim of nickel, ornate plating on the oven door. I remember her heating her iron on a burner for the laundry. I also remember her talking on their crank phone which was mounted on the wall a little too high for her for she had to stand on a box to reach the mouth piece. When she wanted to make a call, she would crank the handle several times and would say something like, "Sarah, get me Hanna." Everything was so different then. How times have changed. Are they for the better? Sometimes I wonder.

Ruth had a neighbor across the dirt road we would occasionally visit. Jessie was so nice and so old fashioned. The last time I saw her I was four, but she made such an impression on me I remember her so vividly. She wore an ankle length calico dress with a ruffled apron tied around her waist and a bonnet covering her gray hair. The bonnet was just like the women wore on the prairie going west. Her shoes were black, laced over the ankles. She had a southern accent which most people have in that part of Ohio. She would always greet us with an elevated, hearty, "Howdy." I liked her a lot. Leaving, afterwards, we walked down her old stone walk passing the hollyhocks that lined the white picket fence. That was the first time I had ever seen hollyhocks. They were very impressive, especially since they were taller than I was. Jessie called to me saying, "Bye Patsy." I turned to her responding with, "Bye Jessie. We'll see you in the mornin." Sadly, I never saw Jessie after that.

Every Sunday we attended their little Bethel church. At that time there wasn't a completed road leading to it, some of it was over bedrock. The church was typical of the little, white, clap-board, country churches with a steeple rising high towards the heavens. Inside was a large potbellied stove positioned in the middle of the room surrounded by maple wood pews and up front was an old pump organ. The scene was like out of a movie, only this was the real thing. Beside the church is the Bethel Cemetery. Great Uncle Ralph and Ruth rest there. Ralph died in an automobile accident when in his seventies and Ruth lived to be 106.

Late in the summer Mother had called and asked Ralph to drop me off at the general store in Beaver. She wanted to take me back on a Greyhound bus. As Uncle Ralph approached the store, I remember seeing her standing on the boardwalk. In my mind I can still see what she wore that day. She wore a white eyelet, ankle length dress, matching white shoes with ankle straps and her wavy blond hair parted in the middle. She broke into a smile when she saw me. When I got out she handed me a tiny bottle of

Jergens Lotion. I was delighted with her gift. Uncle Ralph waved goodbye as he pulled away and I don't remember anything after that. *Thank you Aunt Ruth and Uncle Ralph for taking me in that summer.*

14

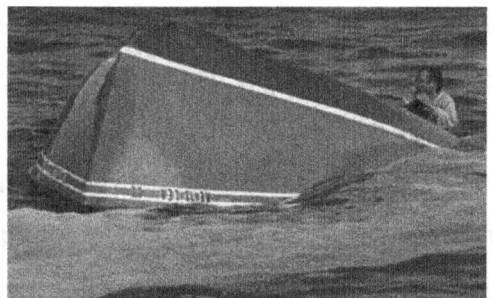

WHERE'S CHARLEY

After the plane crash, Dad didn't have a plane for a while. In that time period he purchased a camp not far from the cottage. It had a main building for the office and several cabins for vacationers and fishermen, many of which were from Ohio. The consistent scenario with fish outings was, and is, a limited time which is usually one or sometimes two weeks to acquire the catch they want which can't be over the limit. The problem that often arises is that the weather is not always conducive for being on a lake, and people who are determined to have their fish to take home often go out in bad weather conditions.

One summer, three men had reservations for one week. The first morning, a low front moved in, bringing light rain and moderate wind. Those conditions were not bad enough to not go out. However, after a couple of hours the storm increased to a very serious intensity. The rain was a high, wind-driven downpour and waves whipped up to a dangerous height, creating conditions that would be treacherous for even much larger boats. Another man from the camp that had been out fishing came in with great difficulty. He hadn't been as far south as the three men, but they were within his vision. Immediately after pulling the camp's boat up on shore he rushed to the office to find Jerry (my dad). Finding him in the office, he asked breathlessly, "Don't you have some men out there?" "Yes," Dad replied. "Well, they're in trouble!"

Not thinking of himself, he immediately went to a neighbor for a larger, steel boat thinking there would be four men coming back in it, plus the steel boat would be safer. He headed the boat toward the south end of the lake. Gowganda Lake is a very large lake with several legs that lead off the main body; even so, he had an approximate idea of their location based upon the information given. The storm had not eased up much so it was a struggle to keep the boat under control. With so much resistance, it would take him longer to reach the men.

He was soaking wet from not taking the time to put on rain gear and was shaking from the chill. After twenty or thirty minutes of struggling with maneuvering the boat through the pounding waves, he spotted two men sitting on the shore. There were supposed to be three. The boat was capsized in the water, the waves pounding it against the rocky shore. Dad said the look of desperation on their faces haunted him for years after. Through the stinging of the wind-driven rain, he shouted, "Where's Charley?" Both men pointed down to the water. In disbelief, Dad said, "What?" hoping they didn't mean on the bottom. Their faces distorted with anguish and because they were so traumatized and couldn't speak, they just nodded, yes. "How long has he been down there?"

One found his voice to say, "About twenty five minutes." Dad had asked because if it had happened maybe five minutes before, he was going down and try to save him. That was my Dad. He knew what he had to do. Making a mental note of the location, he instructed the men to get into the boat. Solemnly, they headed back to camp. It was wrenchingly difficult leaving Charley behind, down there, over night.

The next morning the storm had passed over. As Dad prepared to go back, the two men, filled with grief, with great difficulty explained what had happened. Between the rain and water washing over the boat, it was collecting too much water. Charley was trying to bail, and getting up, he shifted in the boat causing it to capsize. No doubt the high waves hitting against the boat sideways contributed to the capsizing. Charley had on a heavy jacket, rain gear, plus boots and he couldn't swim. They said he went down like a heavy rock and never came back up.

The raging storm prevented the men from trying to help Charley. To this day, I shudder to think about that dreadful scene and writing about it is truly depressing. Ben Kurky who lived in Gowganda, had a dragging outfit so he and my Dad went back to the location the next day and proceeded with their grim chore of retrieving Charley. It took three drags before they found him. They brought him back to the cottage dock and laid him there covered by a tarp. It was two hours before the authorities came into town for him. All this was very difficult for Dad, especially having to inform Charley's family.

15

THE BICENTENNIAL

Six years after the plane crash was the bicentennial of our country's founding, a memorable year of celebration. David would be six in October; Doug turned sixteen and earned his pilot's license. He could fly before he could drive his dad's car. Dad had sold his business and was happily living in Gowganda from May through September. The bicentennial brought in all four of the Goodyear Blimps. What a rare sight that was as they flew over the Akron area. People at home hurried to their yards to witness something they would probably never see again. People in cars pulled over to the side of the road and got out to watch them.

I've seen the Blue Angels at the Cleveland Air Show and they are certainly exciting to see. The blimps aren't exactly the Blue Angels, but can also be a visual treat. I always enjoyed going to the air shows in Cleveland. Duane was a vice president of First National Bank and worked in Commercial Lending. A customer of Duane's always had a loge by the runway and we were always invited to join them. One summer after the Blue Angels performed, the pilots came down the line of loges to greet the people. I was fortunate to be one of them. They were so young and handsome.

Not all of the events that summer were ones of celebration. The newspaper told of a family flying in the east in their private plane that had crashed in a lake and they all perished. My heart filled with sorrow for them wishing they could have been as fortunate as us. At the same time it reminded me of just how grateful we should always be.

Duane's father, Delbert, passed away just before Easter. The Craig family was never the same after that. With his charismatic personality he was the glue that held the family together. He played the mandolin quite well. When Delbert was living and well, I used to say that the Craig farm was like Grand Central Station. He had so much charisma that people were drawn to him. Visitors were always coming and going, even Duane's friends from our church. He had a very deep, resonant voice and when he became enthusiastic in conversation, his voice kept getting louder and louder until it overwhelmed other conversations going on even in the next room. Someone would inevitably have to say, "Delbert, keep it down."

The summers before his passing drew the family together on the holidays. In the summer we would have picnics on the farm. Duane's mother always made homemade ice cream in a hand crank ice cream maker and made the best pies I have ever eaten. There's a real art to making pies like she made them. She grew up on a ranch in the sand hills outside of Ainsworth, Nebraska. Her father was a homesteader and lived in a sod house while they were building the ranch house. It was considered a small ranch at 4,000 acres. Everyone called Mary Marjorie, Tom, because she was such a tomboy. The name stuck and oddly enough, she liked it.

Delbert worked full time at Goodyear (he came from Tennessee) and worked the farm part time. The farm is one hundred acres in Portage County. It has good soil for growing crops, but his primary income from the farm were the white face cattle. Duane's younger brother Harvey and his wife Marjanna now own the farm, making it the second generation on the land.

With the fourth of July approaching I could see that no one was making plans for a family get-together, so I decided I would have it at our home and hope that some would join us. I included my mother and Douglas. Dad was in Canada. Most of the family did join us, but understandably, it was a little somber. Everyone tried to make the best of it – with one exception.

Three days after the fourth, the phone rang. It was Mother. Her paranoia had set in again. She often had terrible, irrational spells where she thought there was a conspiracy against her, and in her mind, I was the conspiring culprit in most instances. It usually took three days for the pressure, like a volcano, to build up in her mind before it exploded. I would listen and let her vent, sometimes trying to reason with her, but those were always futile efforts. Prior to this incident, I had only one facet of understanding her problem. Another facet dawned on me during this encounter. After asking her many times to tell me exactly what I did or said and not getting an answer, I realized there was nothing. It was all in her imagination. She just kept ranting and screaming. Being with her was always like walking on eggshells, always trying to be careful with everything I said or did.

Not being able to ever resolve these ragings was so exasperating for me. This one in particular upset me. After hanging up the phone, I literally yelled out, "Father, I can't take this anymore, please help me." Immediately he said to my mind, "You have been praying all these years for her to change. She is not going to change. You have to change." OH! Yes, I see that is the way it has to be. That makes sense. Afterwards there was a measure of healing and understanding. *Thank you, heavenly Father, for your divine revelation.*

Many years later, I had a conversation with a psychiatrist who had the opportunity to observe Mother. She called wanting some input from me about Mother. I told her how I had tried in different ways to get through to her and how fruitless and frustrating it was. Her answer was very brief and to the point: "Well, stop, because nothing is going to work. You're just upsetting yourself needlessly." That moment created a sense of release and relief for me and an additional extension of healing. But the longing for a normal, loving, nurturing relationship would never be fulfilled.

16

CLOSED IN

David started spending part of his summers with his Grampa at the age of eleven. Dad wanted him for the entire summer and would plead his case for that every summer, but we just couldn't consent to doing that. We wanted our time with him as well. Dad would try getting Dave to help in the garden, earning his keep, so to speak. Dave would pull a couple of weeds and then disappear. I'm sure his reasoning was, why would a boy want to pull weeds when he had so many ways to keep himself entertained? He had the boat with a nine horse-power motor, a canoe, a four-wheeler, plus swimming, fishing, and flying with Grampa. There were also times when they could go blueberry picking on a burn where blueberries thrive. A burn, as the natives call it, is where there has been a forest fire. Mother would make blueberry pies and pancakes that both Grampa and grandson enjoyed.

Grampa also enjoyed camping in the wilderness and knew there might not be another chance to go camping with Dave, so they made plans to fly back and camp for a couple of days. He loaded the plane with all the food, camping, and fishing equipment needed for the trip and off they went heading north. Before leaving, he told Burt where they were going and how many days they were planning to stay and when they would be back. This is done in the event that they didn't show as scheduled, another pilot would fly back to check on them.

Dad flew to the spot he had previously designated for their campsite. Early in the summer he had taken a boat back to be used later. It had a nice beach that would be good for an approach for the pontoons.

Alongside the beach was a level span of bedrock covered with moss, making a perfect camping spot. The backdrop, as always, was white bark birch trees mixed with pines. The lake was known to usually be good for fishing unless the weather was bad causing the barometer to drop. Then fish won't bite on any lake.

They set up camp and put in some time on the lake that day with some success in catching a couple of nice sized pickerel. Dave enjoyed some time wading and skipping flat-shaped stones in the water. A constant essential was mosquito repellent, and lots of it. When they got up the next morning a low front had moved in; it was a very low front with heavy, dark clouds that meant rain at any minute. They waited all day hoping it was going to lift, but it didn't. Wanting to kill time they played 500 Rummy. They played it many times and being a good Grampa, Dad would occasionally let Dave win...occasionally.

The second day hadn't changed. The rain stopped, but the clouds were still too low for flying, more playing Rummy. Dad said that after that trip he didn't want to ever see a deck of cards again. By the third day the conditions had changed very little, their food had run out and Dad knew that Burt would be a little concerned. By this time a plane would have come back to check on them, however that plane was also grounded due to the weather. Dad and Dave both were understandably growing restless and concern was now growing in Dad's mind. He knew they had to get back and delaying it was going to create other problems.

By mid-afternoon the low hanging clouds had lifted a little, to about 150 feet above the tree tops. It wouldn't be high enough for him to see distant landmarks, but he knew which way he could go to eventually find the road. His intention was to follow that road back to Gowganda. There's only one road in that area, so there would be no confusion in finding the right road. If they found one it would be the one and only.

They took off, just clearing the treetops, and turned in the direction of finding the road. He had to fly uphill and downhill just staying above the tree tops. Dad gripped the wheel tightly and leaned forward into the windshield. It was profoundly intense, maintaining constant and complete control of the plane, following the ever changing terrain with the trees just feet below the pontoons. One wrong reflex could be disastrous. He had to be flying over 50 mph or the plane could stall.

The cloud coverage started dropping again and, flying by a lake, he decided to set down there for the night. Landing, he spotted a couple of cabins on the shore line. In the Canadian wilderness, it is the custom to provide shelter for anyone who is in need of it in an emergency situation. They pulled up to the dock and secured the plane. Dad and Dave both approached the cabin, climbing up slippery wood steps set in a steep bank. They could see lights in the windows. Dad gave a sigh of relief and told Dave, "It's good that we've found someone here. It could have been vacant." A man came to the door and Dad told him that they had been camping and the weather closed in on them. They were trying to get back to Gowganda, but couldn't go any further and needed a place to stay overnight. In disbelief the man refused to let them in. He didn't even offer them something to drink. He must have been a hermit and didn't trust people. Dad didn't know and I can't even guess what his problem was.

He saw Dave who was twelve at the time. How could anyone turn away a man with a young boy under those circumstances? It was unbelievable and most certainly not the norm. It wasn't as though there were dozens of cabins on the lake from which to approach. There were only two. Dad, being perturbed, turned from the man without saying anything and left. Dad explained to Dave, "You mustn't judge all people up here by that man. I've always known the people to go out of their way to help, particularly under these kinds of circumstances."

Getting back into the plane, they taxied down the lake to the other end to the only other cabin. Dad was glad to see interior lights on. Not knowing how they were going to be greeted this time, Dad was a little apprehensive while still stewing about the other inhospitable man. He wanted to be encouraging for Dave's sake. "Now Dave, you watch, we're going to get a good reception this time." Dave handled it all rather well, but the tension from the uncertainty of their situation was noticeably setting in.

This time, when Dad knocked on the door, two friendly, smiling faces greeted them. When Dad started to explain his plight a second time, he was interrupted by the man explaining, "We saw your plane land and watched as you were turned away by our neighbor. We have to apologize for his bad manners. He isn't friendly with us either. We call him 'Herman the Hermit,'" he said jokingly.

"Please come in. I'm Tom and this is my wife Edna." Tom and his wife Edna were actually glad for the company. Edna explained, "We rarely have any visitors here. Occasionally we'll go to Gowganda for supplies. We've seen your plane there on the north shore. It's so rare to have a plane land on our lake. It's exciting to see. I was just getting ready to prepare something for dinner. We have plenty and would be pleased to have you join us. You must be hungry."

Dad responded "Well, we are kind of hungry. We haven't had anything to eat today. Thank you for the offer." Dave was hoping his Grampa would accept. He was starved.

While Edna was preparing dinner, Dad and Tom conversed, mainly about fishing and the cabin, when it was built and their search for the antiques to fill the rooms. It had two bedrooms, a modest sized kitchen and living room. It was an A-frame with a loft that had a ladder to access it.

Dad started noticing the features of the room. It had a nice sized, picture window that looked out onto the lake. The walls, ceiling, and kitchen cabinets were of warm knotty pine. Rough hewn beams crossed from one wall to the other. The floor was of wide plank boards and partially covered with a braided rug in warm, earthy colors that blended harmoniously with the wood tones. They sat in two comfortable antique rockers that creaked with every rock. On the back wall was a striking stone fireplace with a log fire. The weather front had caused the temperature to drop into the fifties, so the warmth from the fire was a welcome touch. Over the fire place hung the largest pickerel Dad had ever seen. Hung right in the middle was a moose rack that stretched the entire width of the fireplace. Dad said he was in a backwoods paradise.

As Edna announced that dinner was ready, she opened the front door and called, "Margaret, dinner's ready." A young girl about twelve rushed up the front steps, crossed the kitchen to the sink and washed her hands before quickly sitting down at the table next to Dave. Not being shy and smiling broadly she said, "Hi, I'm Meg. What's your name?" Edna said in a somewhat stern way, letting Meg know that she was to wait for an introduction. "Margaret, this is, David Craig, and his grandfather, Jerry Dever."

Dave said she wore her dark hair in pigtails, was dressed like a boy, and a little too forward for him. However, her effervescent personality soon coaxed him out of his timidity, and they were soon chatting like old friends. They talked about fishing, camping and boating – Dave's favorite subjects at the time. He took her down to see the plane allowing her to sit in the pilot's seat. She was all excited about that when relaying it to her mother. Everyone enjoyed the hot cocoa Edna very thoughtfully made and served before retiring for the night. Dad was exhausted and Dave could hardly keep his eyes open. All that Tom and Edna afforded them was comforting and appreciated, but all the time Dad was concerned about the next day and what it would bring. *Thank you, Tom and Edna.*

17

FOLLOW THE ROAD

The following morning, after getting a good night's rest, the first in three days, Edna served them a hearty, hot breakfast, including her biscuits made in her antique iron skillet. They were a treat for Dad and Dave, especially topped with her homemade blueberry jam. Finishing his coffee, Dad thanked them for their very gracious and generous hospitality.

Checking outside, he was disappointed to see the weather still had not improved. It looked like his plan would still have to be to follow the road. Tom informed Dad that their drive led to the road about 800 feet west of the cabin. Dad said he would like to come back and give Tom and Edna a ride to another lake for an afternoon of fishing. They liked that idea and accepted the offer. Thanking Tom and Edna one more time, they took off heading west of the cabin and upon spotting the road, they turned south. Dad felt a lot better than the day before, having slept all night and getting a good breakfast, but the stress of having to still fly over the tree tops was not any better and he said the thought of it was unnerving. He knew he still had to follow the road.

At one point, he flew into a dense fog not being able to see anything for maybe thirty seconds. That had to be terrifying. He said later, it did cause some trepidation. Fortunately, at the time, they were flying over level terrain. When they came out of it Dave said, "Whew!" with a loud sigh of relief. "That was scary Grampa!"

There were many places where the road had been cut through the hills and Dave said he remembers looking up and seeing trees above the plane. Dad had to fly that close to the road and at that time, it was not very wide. That took a lot of skill and self control. Because the intensity was so stressful, Dad decided to set down one more time and rest for a while before tackling the last part of the flight. When they finally came over Gowganda, they could see Burt waiting at the dock. They were home at last. "That'a way Grampa!" Dave shouted, giving him a high five. Burt had heard the plane coming in and was at the dock to grab the strut and secure the plane. "I didn't expect you to come in through this soup. You must have run out of food," he said jokingly. "Actually," Dad said, "I got tired of losing at rummy." Everyone laughed.

They survived because of
THE GOWGANDA PILOT.

18

BIG HEART, BIG TROUBLE

David graduated from high school in 1989. We planned a graduation celebration for him inviting classmates and family. My dad was already in Canada and we really didn't expect him to drive the distance for the event, but he was so faithful to David, he told me he was going to be there. No matter how much I tried to convince him not to make that long trip, the more determined he was in his decision. I asked Dave to call his Grampa and try to reason with him, but his mind was set. "I'm going to be there," he said emphatically. This concerned me and I couldn't get it out of my mind. I kept thinking I wish he wouldn't do this because I knew how he made these trips in one day, pressing on at top speed. Dad was seventy one at the time.

As it turned out, the party was not what I had hoped it to be. Unbeknownst to me, Dave had erroneously told his classmates not to come because it was just for family. Disappointingly, most of Duane's family didn't show for various reasons. We had an abundance of food left over that fed us for twenty days. But, true to his word, Dad was there. God bless his big, loyal heart. His big heart got him into big trouble. On his trip back to Gowganda, he was again determined to make it in one day even though we had asked him to please make it a two day trip. Doing this in one day was too risky. Duane and I did it once and it's too risky. Why not make it an easier effort by breaking the driving time in half? Stay overnight somewhere and be refreshed the next morning, ready for the last six hundred miles or so. Pushing it like he always did was about to catch up with him.

About two hours north of North Bay and having the cruise control set on 70 mph, he fell asleep at the wheel. His truck went left of center and off the left side of the road, steadily climbing up a hill. The road had been cut into the hill curving left through it. As his truck climbed to the crest it flew off the cliff, rolled in the air, landing upside down on the highway crushing the top flat to the front seat.

In some miraculous way, he was flung to the floor. How, no one knows or has speculated. Obviously, he couldn't have had his seat belt buckled. If he had, he wouldn't have survived. In no way am I undermining the importance of seat belts. Statistics prove that they are extremely effective in reducing injuries and fatalities. However, in this case the belt would have been fatal for him. All that aside, due to the horrific state of the truck afterwards, no one could believe he survived. *Thank you, Father, for this additional survival.*

A semi happened to be following Dad a short distance behind and pulled off the road. He ran to see how he could help. Knelling down and peering inside, he could barely see Dad tightly pinned in. He could tell Dad was alive by sounds he was making. The driver was unable to communicate with Dad as he was in and out of consciousness. The driver went back to his truck to get some cutting tools. By that time another car stopped and the passenger was a nurse named Nancy. She called to Dad, "Who can I call to notify someone in your family?" In his grogginess and pain he incredibly remembered my number because he called it most often.

A short distance south was a phone booth that stood beside a small store that hadn't opened yet. It was seven a.m. Nancy drove quickly to that phone. I had been out for my early morning walk and just as I opened the door, I heard the phone ringing. I have often thought, what if I had arrived home later, I would have missed that call. It was Nancy on the other end. She told me what had happened and that she had to hurry back to be with Dad, but would call later with more information. I thanked her for stopping to help and I said I would stay close to the phone waiting for her next call. Next, I called Mother and Duane, telling them to stand by.

By the time, Nancy returned to Dad the truck driver was frantically struggling with the door, to cut it open or off, I'm not sure. It was jammed from extensive buckling from the impact. Nancy later explained what had transpired. It took the truck driver a full hour to finally cut through. He and Nancy carefully pulled Dad out onto a grassy berm. Nancy stayed with Dad keeping the mosquitoes off him by fanning him with a magazine and periodically taking his pulse. She kept trying to console him and keep him conscious by getting him to talk. That couldn't have been easy. Ironically, Nancy lived in northern Ohio, east of Cleveland. She was Canadian and had married a Yankee. She was heading north to visit relatives. We kept in touch for a few years. I wish now we had continued that connection.

The truck driver had called police and an ambulance, both of which had to come all the way from North Bay – a two-hour drive. I wish I knew the truck driver's name. It's unfortunate that I don't know it. He left the scene before the police arrived. I was told it was for some legal reason. *Thank you, Nancy and unknown truck driver.*

A patrolman arrived first and did his best to console Dad. Nancy was still there and said the patrolman was very compassionate and helpful. The ambulance arrived and transported him to the hospital at North Bay. By noon that same day, Mother, Duane, Dave, and I quickly packed a few clothes and took off for Canada. We all took turns driving Mother's new car. She would get a little uptight when Dave was taking his turn. He had just received his driver's license at eighteen and that made her very nervous, especially when he made his turns too close and the tires scraped the curbs.

Early in the spring of that year Dad had purchased that new, royal blue Ford pick-up and it was a beauty. Somehow, someone in Gowganda was notified and Dad's friends came down to salvage his belongings from the truck. One of them took a picture of the truck. I am impressed when I think of the kind of loyal men that were his friends. *Thank you for being so considerate of Dad.*

When we finally arrived at the hospital we took turns going into the intensive care unit. When I walked into the room I was horrified at what I saw. He was unrecognizable: his head and face were badly swollen, his cheek-bones were shattered, he had a severe concussion, broken ribs, a collapsed lung, and other injuries. The staff said it was a miracle he survived. I believed it because his life had been filled with miracles. However, up to then, Dad had never recognized that.

The long ride back to Ohio was quiet and somber. I don't remember any conversation. Dad was in ICU for an extended duration of which I don't remember. One day after he was placed in a room and able to speak, he had a nurse dial my number so he could talk to me. He still remembered my phone number. When he first spoke, I didn't recognize his voice. It startled me when I realized who it was. It didn't sound at all like him. My hands were shaking as I pulled up a chair to sit while I listened. He began with, "I know what I'm going to do with the rest of my life." Tears flowed down my cheeks as I listened. Dad had always been an agnostic, never willing to make that step towards his Heavenly Father. It wasn't until then that he recognized how miraculous all the circumstances in his life had been. He survived once again.

When he finally arrived back home, he sang:

Wasted years, wasted years
Oh, how foolish as you walk on
In darkness and fear

Turn around, turn around, God is Calling

He's calling me from a life of wasted years.

There was to be one more miracle in his life.

19

DAVE AND ANGIE

In the summer of 1990, there was a flu virus being passed around. I had it first and then Duane. Shortly after, Dave started having the same symptoms, but they hung on too long and after five days I could see that it was more than the flu. I told Duane we should take him to the ER. The first ER we took him to, decided he needed to go to City Hospital. They said they were very concerned about our son's condition. There were two different paramedics representing two different services that couldn't decide who was going to take him. In our minds this went on too long. Duane was increasingly growing agitated with them and increasingly concerned for Dave whose condition was getting increasingly worse. Finally, one paramedic made his move and decided he was going to take Dave. Thank heavens.

Upon being examined by the emergency doctor at City Hospital we were informed that Dave had a ruptured appendix and his life was in danger. The doctor called a surgeon who was sound asleep because by now it was 1:30 a.m. By 2:00 a.m. Dave was in surgery. After waiting in the ER lounge for four hours the surgeon came in to give us his report. He said that the appendix must have been ruptured for three days or more because of the extent of the infection. It had spread throughout the abdominal area and it took some time to thoroughly clean it all out. He also said that he was dangerously close to the point of no return. If it had happened just four years before he would not have survived. I didn't ask him why, but I assume it was because of more recent techniques or medications. We thanked the doctor for his dedication and professionalism. *Thank you, Father, for another survival.*

By September, Dave was still weak and not fully recovered, but able to continue his classes at The University of Akron, eventually graduating in 1994 with a Bachelor's degree in corporate communications. He then decided that he wanted to earn his Masters Degree at The Philadelphia Biblical University, where he studied psychology/counseling and Bible. It was our turn to experience the empty nest syndrome and it was very difficult for us.

Dave is a musician and during his college years at The University of Akron, he was the worship leader of the College Class at The Chapel. There were times when they would have jam sessions at our house. Our home was always lively with the happy sounds of his friend's frequent visits. I loved this phase of my life as it was so fulfilling. When Dave left in August of 1994, it sounds strange to say, but it was like the house had died. *Thank you, Father for the good things in life. Help me to always have a grateful heart for Your blessings.*

Dave met the love of his life, Angie Parks, at the university. A few years later, Angie shared with me how she was attracted to him. Dave had caught her eye and timed going to the library exactly when he would be there. She would slowly walk by his table with the intent of catching his eye. She did. We ladies have to give these matters a wee bit of assistance.

Duane and I drove to Langhorne which is where the university is located, to be there for his graduation in May of 1996. After several conversations with different people, I told Duane I would meet him in the car. After a short wait I looked up and saw him hustling to the car. Once in the car, he was so excited about something that I could not understand a word of what he was saying. I told him to slow down and start over. I had never seen him like that. Normally, he is so composed. With some effort to overcome his giddy excitement, he said, "Dave is coming to the car and there's a pretty blond walking behind him and I think she's with him. I hope, I hope." Sure enough, she was indeed with him. Dave introduced us to Angie, the pretty blond and our future daughter-in-law.

Angie graduated one year after Dave. It was then they married, holding the wedding in New Town which is in Bucks County. It was a lovely wedding in a lovely setting. At the reception, the bride and groom made their late entrance. Dave was carrying Angie in his arms and wearing an Indiana Jones hat while the DJ played the theme music from *The Raider of the Lost Ark*. It made quite a hit with the guests. We still talk about it.

I love the villages in Bucks County. They have preserved the historical architecture of their communities and are so very charming and beautiful in my eyes. You see many homes and shops that have used the sand stone from the area because it was available and plentiful. Bucks County is a wonderful area to explore. A few years before, a designer friend of mine and I had gone to that area to search for antiques for clients. We included a couple of architectural salvage places which were filled with all kinds of interesting things that had been taken from old buildings before being torn down. We stayed in a little B&B in New Hope along the Delaware River.

I would never have guessed then that someday Dave would be living in Bucks County.

Dave and Angie found a historical home in Langhorne, built in 1686 on Olde Lincoln Highway. If one thinks about that, that's before George Washington was born. At some point in time it had been divided into several apartments and they had the smallest one. Maybe I should say the tiniest one. Johnny Carson's audience would now say, "How small was it?" It was so small they could cook on the range, put the milk in the fridge, place food on the table, and wash the dishes without taking a single step. Even so, they were pretty excited about it as it was their first place.

In 2003 they moved to Akron. We were thrilled to have him back home once again. Dave served as worship pastor at The Chapel for the Sunday evening service. The pastor at this time was Knute Larson. By this time Dave and Angie had a son, Drew, who was two, and their fraternal twin girls, Abby and Ashlyn, had just been born in September.

They are now living in the Denver area, deciding it is where they want to stay and I can understand that. The climate is good with little or no humidity; the winters are usually pretty mild and so much is available for shoppers and outdoor enthusiasts. Dave is now marketing coordinator for Apex Recreational Centers in Arvada. One day he overheard a conversation between a father and son playing golf on the Apex golf course. The son's golf ball landed behind a tree which happened to be in direct line to the green. The son looking up at the tree heard his dad say, "You know son, when I was your age, I was in the same predicament at this same tree. You know what I did, I swung at that ball so hard it flew up over the top of the tree and landed on the green right by the cup." So the son thought, "Well if my dad could do that, so can I." He gripped the club and swung as hard as he could. The ball went up in the air, hit a tree branch and tumbled back down to his feet. "Well, that didn't go very well," the son said irritated. "Well, you know son, I didn't mention that the tree was only three years old at the time."

Dave has a wonderful sense of humor. He also loves to ski and snow board and taught his kids to do the same. Angie enjoys skiing, but prefers to run marathons. I should say used to. Now, she has moved on to more challenging runs like the ultra 50 milers. The one she seems to enjoy the most is in Steam Boat Springs. What a beautiful area! Coming down that last mountain and looking down into the valley below is like seeing Shangri-La.

Angie's father, Ron Parks, was a pitcher for the Los Angeles Dodgers minor league until overuse of his arm caused so much pain he had to give up his career. His degree was in teaching with an emphasis on history. He acquired a teaching position at the school where the girls attended in Redondo Beach, California. He also coached cross country track since they participated in those events. One gets the picture here of a very devoted father. He did everything to be with his girls, Angie and her younger sister, Chrissy. Ron ran in the ultra 100 milers. It's difficult for me to imagine anyone doing that. Angie says it is her goal to do the same in memory of her father.

Ron finished an *Ultra 50* in 1990 and was sick and headachy afterwards, as most runners are after such a run. Ron knew this was different than how he usually felt since the problem was not getting better. He went to a doctor who, at first, dismissed his symptoms. Upon Ron's insistence a cat scan was given revealing a malignant brain tumor in the frontal lobe. The doctor recommended immediate surgery. Ron insisted that they take his blood before the surgery. In the event that he needed a blood transfusion, he wanted his own blood. After the surgery, the doctor said they removed as much of the cancer as they could. He went through chemo and radiation treatments and lost all of his beautiful, thick, curly hair. He did go back to teaching and taught for as long as he could.

Angie was thirteen years old at the time. This was devastating for the family as they were very close. Ron took them on many camping trips to the beautiful parks of California. She has seen what I have never seen: the giant redwoods, Yosemite, Bear Mountain, the breath taking Sequoias, and the beautiful drive up the west coast. Those are precious memories for Angie.

Within the same year, the remaining cancer quickly grew and Ron's condition became exceedingly worse. Visiting hospice came every day to their home and did what they could to make him as comfortable as possible. In the middle of one night, Angie's mom, Vicki, woke the girls saying, "It won't be long now before you dad leaves us. You'll want to be with him in his last moments." By his bedside, they prayed together and talked to him telling him how much they loved their papa and what a wonderful papa he was for them. Sadly, Ron never got to see his beautiful grandchildren.

In 2012, Duane and I moved from Akron to be with Dave and his family. We wanted our grandchildren, Ashlyn, Abby, and Drew to have many fond memories of being with their grandparents. They call Gramps, Bop. I think Drew, who is the oldest, once heard Dave call his Dad, Pop, and Drew thought he said Bop. Anyway, it stuck and he will forever be Bop.

20

THE LAST CHAPTER

Sometime in 1993, Dad started slipping into Alzheimer's due to the terrible head trauma suffered in the truck accident in 1989. At the time, we didn't get the connection of his behavior with Alzheimer's and when talking to others who had a loved one with this devastating disease, they would say the same thing; they didn't recognize the connection at first. The statistics indicate that one out of every twelve people will get this dreaded disease.

And, by 2020, it will be one out of every seven. That's scary.

One time while visiting him at his home, he took out a grey metal box and took out the contents which were all greeting cards I had sent him over the years: Christmas, birthdays, father's day, Easter, etc. I was astounded. I had no idea and was deeply touched by the sentimentality behind keeping those cards. I was always particular about each card I chose – something with a lake and cabin or a fisherman in a boat, something appropriate for an outdoorsman. He always showed his appreciation of my selections; I had no idea of just how much. I would have liked to have them back after he passed away, but Mother threw everything of his away afterwards.

I remember Dad sitting in our family room telling us something that had happened recently and the following visit, a few days later, he would tell us the same story. This would be repeated several times. Finally, one day as he was starting to tell the same story again, I said, "Dad, you've told us that story five times already." There was a l-o-n-g moment of silence. "Well...you're going to hear it again." We laughed then and still laugh about it. His sense of humor was still intact.

He would get frustrated at times when trying to tell us something and could not pull the words out of his memory. He would say, "I just can't remember like I used to." It was apparent it upset him as it would anyone. I felt so badly for him. I would try to come up with the word for which he was searching so it wouldn't be so frustrating. He had purchased a new, blue, Ford Windstar and complained that it was pulling to the right. He wanted me to drive it so I could see for myself. "Can you see how it's pulling to the right?" he would ask.

"No, not really Dad." This was before we knew what was happening to him. Once we knew, it was so heart breaking to see the disease as it progressed.

There were three mornings when the phone would ring at 2:00 a.m. or 3:00 a.m. from the State Highway Patrol somewhere in southern Ohio. They would find him off the road somewhere and take him to the station.

His mental compass was taking him south trying to reach his deceased relatives in the Beaver area that he thought were still living. He couldn't remember his home phone number, but he could still remember mine. So, Duane and I would get up in the middle of the night and drive up to 150 miles or so to pick him up. One of us had to drive his car back.

I would tell Mother that she had to hide the keys from him. But, I would find out that he was still driving and we would get another call from southern Ohio. Around town, the police knew him pretty well as they would stop him for going left of center or find him in a ditch. They never cited him which was unfortunate, because had they done so, his license would have been revoked and he would be off the road. They apparently felt sorry for him because he was never given a citation. This continued several times. I asked Mother, "Are you hiding the keys to the van Mother?"

Her response was, "Yes, I hide them in my purse."

"Mother, that isn't hiding them," I responded.

"For his sake and others, you have to be certain he doesn't get those keys. You're responsible for that. One of these days he's going to cause an accident and injure himself or someone else, or both, and possibly have a law suit against you. You don't want that to happen."

I'm not a prophet, by any means, but that is exactly what happened, resulting in a lawsuit against him. He made a left hand turn in front of an oncoming car and left the scene. This was his last survival. After he drove home, Mother saw the badly damaged van and hid it behind some blue spruce at the back of their property. She didn't get away with it though because the police had stopped him so many times, that when the victims described the van and driver, the police knew exactly who it was and where to go. Fortunately, no one was injured in the accident, but the victims still pursued a lawsuit anyway. In my mind suing a man with Alzheimer's and no injuries to anyone was inappropriate. Dad's insurance took care of the damages. Another blow was after Dad passed away they transferred the lawsuit from Dad to Mother who wasn't even in the vehicle at time of the accident. They held her responsible for him having the keys.

A few times he would ask me to trim his hair when it got a little shaggy. As I would be trimming, he would ask, "It's getting pretty long back there isn't it?" I would respond with, "Yes, it is Dad."

About thirty seconds later, "It's getting pretty long back there isn't it?"

"Yes, it is Dad."

I used to always keep ice cream in the freezer for him as he loved Sundays with a chocolate topping. He lost his desire for that and so many other things. He became unaware of his appearance and the need for appropriate clothing and the statements he would make made no sense. This was the man who intelligently ran a successful business, built a summer home, flew airplanes, managed properties, and at the end of his life deteriorated to a vegetable. It's a devastating way to end one's life journey. The inevitable day came when he had to go into a nursing home.

He knew us when he was admitted. When Duane entered his room, he jokingly said, "Hey, there's the old man," but after that, we couldn't believe how quickly he declined. Then, he was gone within a month.

On the 11th of August that year 2001, I had a birthday party for Duane for his 70th birthday. I had to temporarily push the thoughts of my dad aside to make the celebration a happy one. There were about forty people that attended. I rented three pontoon boats so we could all enjoy a cruise around the lakes. The white swans and ducks followed the boats looking for handouts. It was two days after, on the thirteenth that Dad passed away. Mother was notified by the nursing home very early in the morning and chose not to call me then. She called Doug and the two went to the funeral home to make the arrangements for his funeral. When she did call at 2:00 p.m. she said in an irritated tone. "I've been trying to get you all day." "That isn't true Mother, I've been here all day and the phone hasn't rung once," I retorted in an irritated tone. She stammered quite a bit in trying to respond to that.

Mother lived in her own little world. I tried so many times to break through that wall. I often think that perhaps I didn't always go about it in the best or right way, but remembering the words of the psychiatrist, nothing would have worked. I know that our peace and strength cannot come from others or material things. It has to come from within through God's spirit of love and guidance. I believe that because I have experienced it. But sometimes it can take years for problems to be completely or partially resolved and sometimes they are never resolved at all. Either way, we have to rest in Him because He knows what goes on in our lives and He truly cares. I like to sing the song "Dear Jesus, abide in me as I walk life's troubling sea and make my life what it ought to be. Dear Jesus, abide in me."

My prayer is always, "Father, help me to be the kind of person you would have me to be." Those prayers have always been answered.

Mother didn't ask anyone to talk about Dad at the funeral – no eulogies. A few of his friends were still living and would have been so willing to have done so. She could have had my brother or my son David, talk about some of their fishing or camping trips with Dad. The pastor that was asked to officiate was going into Alzheimer's himself and never once mentioned Dad. Instead, he talked the entire time about his own family. No one was interested in his family. Everyone came to hear something about Dad. Even so, I don't I fault that pastor.

Afterwards, Dave said, "I kept waiting and waiting, thinking he would eventually say something, even mention his name. But it never happened." Dave was obviously saddened by this and of course, I was also. Dad was a man that accomplished so much and was generous to others and not a word was spoken about him. Mother passed away in 2009 from a severe stroke at age 90. She and Dad rest in a small cemetery in Copley, Ohio.

EPILOGUE

It was important for me to write this story because I didn't want the memories of my dad to be forgotten. As of this writing, it's been forty-three years since the plane crash. Starting out, I wasn't sure how much I would remember, but as I began, the writing flowed and kept flowing. I was drawn to the keyboard like a moth being drawn to a flame. Details I thought were long forgotten came flooding back from the archives of my mind, like they were anxiously waiting for the opportune moment to jump out onto the pages as I wrote. The experience has been an emotional roller coaster ride, going to the deepest areas of grief and weeping, to the heights of joy and gratitude.

During those days of flying with him and working by his side in his garden in Gowganda, I knew then just how special those moments were. I took great delight in them and savored them. I would think, someday I'll look back on this and say, "Those were wonderful memories and what a unique privilege and experience it was to have shared them with him."

He saved my life that day on August 11, 1970, as well as David's and Duane's. If it hadn't been for his presence of mind, strength, and determination, I wouldn't have had the privilege of seeing our son born, grow up, seeing his graduations, his wedding, his wife and children…or writing this book.

Thank you Daddy. I'm eternally grateful.

He was and will always be, my GOWGANDA PILOT.

THE GOWGANDA PILOT

Verse 1
There once was a pilot who flew the blue northern skies,
A 180 Cessna on floats from the water he would rise, he would rise,
Jerry Dever was his name; he never flew for wealth or for fame,
He loved the great northern wilderness with air so clear and pure,
Many hours he spent fishing for pickerel with rod, line, and lure,
He built a wilderness summer home in which he would live in this land,
Amid the forests green and dense, speckled with lakes of pure water and sand.

Chorus:
Jerry Dever was his name, never once did he fly for wealth or fame.
All his dreams and goals fulfilled, flying free for him could not be stilled.
In his float plane from the water he would rise, rise, rise,
The Gowganda pilot flying the northern skies...the northern skies.

Verse 2
There is a story his daughter tells, from many years ago of a certain day and flight,
The weather was so strange, so quiet and still, it didn't seem altogether right.

With water like a mirror, no ripples to see, a difficult landing pilots did say,
They wished they had known how serious it was for it was a time for all to pray.
Jerry's daughter, her husband and their son to be, a babe in the womb, David was he.
These were the members in the plane, as it circled and descended, he watched the terrain.

Chorus:
Jerry Dever was his name, never once did he fly for wealth or fame.
All his dreams and goals fulfilled, flying free for him could not be stilled.
In his float plane from the water he would rise, rise, rise,
The Gowganda pilot flying the northern skies...the northern skies.

Verse 3
The pontoons caught, flipping the plane into waters so dark and so deep,
They thought for certain their souls, the lakes depth would surely keep.
Trapped with no air to breathe, hanging upside down they struggled to be free.
With presence of mind, determination strong, Jerry kicked and kicked to open the door,
So strongly did he kick, it finally came off and sunk to the lake's deep and dark floor.
Those memories from so long ago, how he saved their lives, we don't want to forget,
For he was and will always be the Gowganda Pilot flying forever and ever so free.

Chorus:
Jerry Dever was his name, never once did he fly for wealth or fame.
All his dreams and goals fulfilled, flying free for him could not be stilled.
In his float plane from the water he would rise...rise...rise,
The Gowganda Pilot now flying Heaven's great skies....
Heaven's great skies.

CPSIA information can be obtained at www.ICGtesting.com
Printed in the USA
LVOW04s0410030914

402104LV00006B/16/P